CHOOSE THE LIFE YOU WANT

* * *

Praise for *Choose the Life You Want*

"With his customary insight, Tal Ben-Shahar lays out the elements of a happier life in short, thought-provoking chapters that will inspire readers both to think more deeply about their lives—and to take action to turn those ideas into reality."

—**Gretchen Rubin**, *New York Times*–bestselling author of *The Happiness Project* and *Happier at Home*

* * *

Praise for *Happier*

"Ben-Shahar, one of the most popular teachers in Harvard's recent history, has written a personal, informed, and highly enjoyable primer on how to become happier. It would be wise to take his advice."

—**Ellen J. Langer**, author of *Mindfulness* and *On Becoming an Artist*

"This fine book shimmers with a rare brand of good sense that is embedded in scientific knowledge about how to increase happiness."

—**Martin E. P. Seligman**, author of *Flourish*

Praise for *Being Happy*

"Ben-Shahar teaches that happiness isn't as elusive as people think."

—***Publishers Weekly***

"*Being Happy* drew me in immediately and kept me captivated for hours. Tal Ben-Shahar seamlessly weaves personal examples, Gladwellian stories, and illuminating research findings to impart a valuable message. Every person concerned with success—and that includes most of us—should read this book."

—**Sonja Lyubomirsky**, author of *The How of Happiness*

"This book will inspire you to realize your innate potential for happiness and awaken the genuine aspiration to change, while avoiding the trap of perfectionism and the unrealistic demands of the ego."

—**Matthieu Ricard**, author of *Happiness: A Guide to Developing Life's Most Important Skill*

"In *Happier*, [Ben-Shahar] invited us to rethink our assumptions about happiness and what it depends on. Now, in *Being Happy*, he invites us to discard the fallacy that the pursuit of 'perfect' is the best indicator of success and happiness."

—**Nathaniel Branden**, author of *The Six Pillars of Self-Esteem*

Also by
TAL BEN-SHAHAR, PhD

Happier, No Matter What:
Cultivating Hope, Resilience, and Purpose in Hard Times

Short Cuts to Happiness:
Life-Changing Lessons from My Barber

Being Happy:
You Don't Have to Be Perfect to Lead a Richer, Happier Life

Even Happier:
A Gratitude Journal for Daily Joy and Lasting Fulfillment

The Pursuit of Perfect:
How to Stop Chasing Perfection and Start Living a Richer, Happier Life

Happier:
Learn the Secrets to Daily Joy and Lasting Fulfillment

CHOOSE THE LIFE YOU WANT

The Mindful Way to Happiness

TAL BEN-SHAHAR, PHD

AMARYLLIS

AMARYLLIS

An imprint of Manjul Publishing House Pvt. Ltd.
• C-16, Sector 3, Noida, Uttar Pradesh 201 301, India
Website: www.manjulindia.com

Registered Office:
• 2nd Floor, Usha Preet Complex, 42 Malviya Nagar,
Bhopal 462 003 – India

Distribution Centres
Ahmedabad, Bengaluru, Chennai, Hyderabad,
Kochi, Kolkata, Mumbai, Noida, Pune

Choose The Life You Want - The Mindful Way to Happiness
by Tal Ben-Shahar, PhD

Originally published in the United States in 2013 by The Experiment, LLC.
This edition published by arrangement with The Experiment, LLC.

This paperback edition first published in India in 2026

ISBN 978-93-7317-957-5

Cover design by Christine Van Bree
Text design by Pauline Neuwirth, Neuwirth & Associates, Inc.

Printed and bound in India by Repro India Limited

To my parents

Contents

Introduction

One's philosophy is not best expressed in words; it is expressed in the choices one makes. In the long run, we shape our lives and we shape ourselves. The process never ends until we die. And, the choices we make are ultimately our own responsibility.

—Eleanor Roosevelt

For over a decade I have been writing and lecturing in positive psychology, bringing ideas from the "science of happiness" to college students, at-risk populations, corporate executives, and government leaders. Ever since I started on this path, the goal of my work has been to translate rigorous research from the social sciences into accessible and actionable ideas that can help individuals, organizations, and communities flourish.

My initial interest in positive psychology came from my own desire to lead a happier, more fulfilling life. For me, a key component of well-being has always been achieving a reasonable level of work/life balance, and over the years I had found ways to more or less strike this balance. Then the financial crisis hit.

Banks were failing, once thriving companies were barely surviving, funding for programs was drying up, and people were losing their home and livelihood. Even among those who were fortunate enough not to have taken a severe hit, many were losing confidence in a world that no longer seemed as stable and secure. More than ever, my clients needed what positive psychology could offer—help in building resilience, in maintaining the motivation that can sustain individuals and organizations through the difficult times, and, wherever possible, in bringing hidden opportunities to light.

I found I couldn't say no to clients in crisis, and the balance that until then I had been able to maintain between my personal and professional lives was lost. I was consulting to a high-tech company in Paris, delivering a workshop to doctors in Hong Kong, lecturing at a New York high school, participating in a brainstorming session about the changing market in Tel Aviv—generally appearing wherever and whenever I thought positive psychology could help mitigate some of the effects of the crisis. Even when I was at home, I was regularly having conference calls across time zones long into the night.

After a year of going more or less nonstop, I was exhausted and burnt out. I realized just how drained I was one night, while preparing to lead an intensive three-day program, one that I knew would require me to push my clients hard to find the delicate balance between realism and optimism, between acknowledging a painful present and envisioning a brighter future. Usually I am excited about taking up a new challenge, but this time I was not looking forward to it at all. I simply could not imagine how I would get through the next few days.

I tried to give myself a little pep talk. But this time it didn't work, and neither did the other methods and techniques that had helped me in the past. I had no energy, and no motivation. It seemed that if I wanted to go ahead with the program, the only option was to simply force myself through it. I had done it before, and I could do it again. I would have to. I had no choice.

With this uninspiring thought, I went to bed feeling even worse. Not only was I unhappy about what the days ahead seemed to hold in store, I was disappointed in my own failure to imagine a more inspired solution to the problem. I hadn't solved the problem, I had simply resigned myself to living with it. And then, just as I was drifting into sleep, I thought, *No, it's not true that I just have to suffer through the next few days. I have a choice!*

In that moment I realized that to a great extent how I would experience the next three days was up to me. I could choose the path of simply suffering through it or I could choose an alternative path—one where I would draw energy from enthusiastic participants, from engaging in material I passionately believe in, and from reconnecting to my personal mission to make the world a better place through education. Choosing between the path of misery and the path of energetic engagement was a no-brainer.

Once I made my choice, I changed my focus. And by changing my focus I changed my feelings. A few minutes earlier I had felt trapped, but now I was actually excited about the next few days. I was fired up, and went on to deliver one of the most passionate performances of my life.

As soon as I realized what my options were, I made my decision in a split second. But getting to the point where I realized I had options was significantly more difficult. In other words, the choice was made possible—and obvious—only as soon as I became mindful of the fact that I actually had a choice. We are used to thinking of making decisions as the hard part. But the truth is that often the more difficult thing is realizing that there is a decision to be made, that we have a choice.

In fact, at every moment in our life we have a choice.

* * *

Maybe this realization shouldn't have come as such a surprise to me. After all, research in psychology illustrates that about 40 percent of our happiness is determined by the choices that we make—what we choose *to do* and how we choose *to think* directly impact the way *we feel.*

For instance, if I am passed over for a promotion at work or if a new business venture fails, I can decide to treat this experience either as a severe blow from which I may never recover or as a wake-up call—an opportunity to learn and to grow. If I choose to see it only as a negative, I will feel bad about myself and pessimistic about my future. But if I choose to see it as a wake-up call, I can begin to draw lessons from this setback and to improve my prospects for the future. Realizing that I have a choice to make not only improves the likelihood of success in the future, but it will also make me feel better right now, in the present.

In his well-known poem "The Road Not Taken," Robert Frost describes standing at a fork in the road. Forced to choose between two different paths, Frost famously opted for the road that was less traveled—a choice that, in the long run, "made all the difference" in his life.

The drama of Frost's personal dilemma—the difficulty in deciding which path to take, knowing that the effect of this choice would reach far into the future—resonates with every reader. We have all been there: having to decide whether to commit to a particular relationship, what major to declare in college, whether to accept a job offer in another city, and so on. In these difficult moments we try hard to make the right decision, doing our best not to be paralyzed by our own awareness of just how important it is to make the right choice, knowing that not to choose is in itself a choice with far-reaching consequences.

But the dramas of life's "big decisions" (which, almost by definition, are few and far between) should not hide the fact that in life we face choices all the time. *Every moment of our waking life* we face choices whose cumulative effect on us is just as great, if not greater, than the effect of the big decisions. I can choose whether to sit up straight or stooped; whether to say a warm word to my partner or give her a sour look; whether to appreciate my health, my friend, and my lunch, or to take them all for granted; whether to choose to choose or to remain oblivious to the choices that are there for the making. Individually, these choices may not seem important, but together they are the very bricks that make up the road we create for ourselves.

Moreover, choices can create momentum by launching a chain reaction—a series of events or feelings—whose impact is far greater than what you can foresee at the moment the choice is made. For example, if I feel gloomy and weary in the morning, I can decide to improve my mood by taking a few deep breaths, smiling, or bringing the spirit of play to whatever it is that I'm doing. Any of these choices can create a positive chain reaction, putting me in a cheerful mind-set that lasts the entire day and triggers other positive experiences at work and home. Similarly, deciding to make an effort and truly listen to what a person has to say when first we sit down for a meal together can positively impact the quality of the entire conversation, and even the relationship as a whole.

Often, because we can't see that we are at a fork in the road—that these choices in fact exist—we are unable to take advantage of them. Henry Ford once remarked, "Whether you think you can or can't—you are right." The same applies to choices: Whether you think you have a choice or not—you are right. In other words, the fact that you think that you don't have a choice, actually makes it so. The night before my lecture, when I felt exhausted and uninspired, I saw only one way to make it through the next few days. My limited perspective at that moment limited my options.

Not to be aware of the choices we make moment by moment, is to relinquish control over our ability to improve our life. For instance, we take it for granted that our feelings are what they are and cannot be altered; we react to someone else's behavior automatically without considering alternative options; we are faced with the same situation over and over again and respond in the same way over and over again—as if no other course of action were available to us. We assume that our thoughts and actions and feelings are inevitable, that we do not have a choice, when in fact we do.

In *The Way of the Peaceful Warrior,* Dan Millman recounts a story that he heard from his mentor:

> When the lunch whistle blew, all the workers would sit down together to eat. And every day, Sam would open his lunch pail and start to complain. "Son of a gun!" he'd cry, "Not peanut butter and jelly sandwiches again. I hate peanut butter and jelly!" He whined about his peanut butter and jelly sandwiches day after day after day until one of the guys on the work crew finally said, "Fer crissakes, Sam, if you hate peanut butter and jelly so much, why don't you just tell yer ol' lady to make you something different?"
>
> "What do you mean, my ol' lady?" Sam replied. "I'm not married. I make my own sandwiches."

So many of us, without even noticing that we are doing so, make our own sandwiches with ingredients we do not like. Life presents us with raw materials—external circumstances that are sometimes out of our control, such as our physical attributes, the family that we're born into, the fluctuations of global markets, or choices that other people make and that we have no say in. And yet, even with all the limitations and constraints, which raw materials we select and how we decide to use them is to a great extent up to us.

All of us, regardless of the circumstances we find ourselves in, can make a conscious effort to search for possibilities around and within ourselves. And when we look beyond our habitual ways of seeing things, we are often surprised by the many delicious ingredients from which we can choose to make our own sandwiches. Our freedom to choose among the raw materials as well as among different possible responses to any given situation makes us *cocreators of our reality*.

So what kind of reality do you want to create for yourself? The sandwiches that you eat are largely of your own making. You have more choices than you realize. It is up to you, to choose.

What This Book Is and Isn't

THE AHA MOMENT THAT I had the night before the workshop made me realize that I could be playing a much more active role in creating the kind of life that I want for myself. By making a deliberate effort to expose possibilities that I would have previously overlooked, I opened up a world of opportunities. This small change in perspective had a major impact on my life. And that is why I decided to write this book.

The book comprises three types of choices: first, the choices we have at almost every moment, such as whether we smile or whether we take in a deep breath; second, choices that we have following a specific event, such as how we react to failure or whether we choose to compliment a colleague on a job well done; third, choices that relate to the big decisions in life, such as about the career path we decide to pursue or whether we choose to help and contribute to others. The book focuses mostly on the first two types of choices, although a few of the third kind are sprinkled throughout.

This is not a book about ethical decision making or about providing you with tools for making other types of difficult decisions. Most of the choices in this book—just like most of the choices we face in life—are ones that I would describe as "rhetorical choices"; in other words, choices where it is very clear and obvious which path is the right one to take. Most of the time, we know exactly what is good and what isn't—whether it's about the way we sit or walk, the way we respond to failure or success, the way we communicate with our child or partner—and yet very often we do not practice what we know is good for us. Socrates's claim that "to know the good is to do the good" is, unfortunately, not true.

This book is not about decision making in the sense of knowing what is right, but about decision making in the sense of *doing* what is right. Toward this end, I have two objectives: First, to help you become *mindful* of the actual choices that exist in your life minute by minute and day by day; to choose to do what is right, you have to be aware of the fact that there is a choice to make. Second, to encourage you to *act* in the best possible way in light of these choices that are available to you; to do the good once you know the good.

The book is structured as a series of choices, most of them rhetorical choices. Following each choice is a quote, a brief explanation of the choice, and a story that illustrates the choice. The stories include personal anecdotes, hypothetical situations, descriptions of psychological experiments, accounts of historical figures, and experiences of fictional figures from film or literature. The purpose of the story following each choice is to bring the ideas to life and make them more accessible and relatable. It is up to you to generalize the particular examples and apply them to other situations in your own life. For example, if the story has to do with the workplace, you may want to consider how that particular choice is relevant to your home life; if it describes a relationship with your partner, think about a similar situation relating to your boss or child.

You can read the book as you would any other book. Or you can treat it like a workbook—dedicating anywhere between a day to a month to *reflect* and *act* on each of the choices. It may be helpful to you if you write down the choice you're focusing on and place it somewhere where you'll be reminded of it—on your fridge or desk, in your pocket, or on your mobile device or computer as a screen-saver. A form of reminder that I've found most useful—which has helped me get a choice ingrained, making it second nature—is a simple string that I tie around my wrist, wearing it as a wristband for anywhere between a week and a month (psychologist William James claimed that it takes twenty-one days to form a new habit). Currently I have a wristbrand reminding me to bring humor and lightness to situations; before that, during a stressful period in my life, I had a wristband reminding me to be more patient with my kids.

As you read through the book, try out the different choices. If, after some deliberation or some experimentation, a particular choice does not speak to you at all, skip to the next one, or repeat a choice that you have already dealt with. Return to the choice that you skipped at a later date, to see whether something is there for you after all.

You may want to select a few of the choices in the book as a subject for discussion at your book club, or among your family and friends. In the workplace, meaningful discussions about choices can increase the cohesiveness and effectiveness of a team as well as provide an antidote to the kind of rigid thinking that so often stifles innovation. Sharing personal stories about the choices that have shaped our life can be an extremely powerful experience that often inspires action.

Some of the choices that I present in this book are derived from my own experience and those of friends and clients; others are based on the work of psychologists, philosophers, and leaders from the worlds of business and education. Wherever relevant, an endnote will guide you to sources where the ideas originated or are developed in greater depth.

You will find that there is some overlap among the choices in this book. This is an intentional choice on my part, and for two reasons: first, because sometimes approaching the same challenge from different angles helps us get unstuck and change our habits; and second, because repetition is crucial if we want to ensure that the changes we make actually stick.

Thank you for choosing to read this book.

Choice is creation.
To choose is to create.
Through my choices I create my reality.

⁂ ⁂ ⁂

At every moment in my life I have a choice.
Moments add up to a lifetime; choices add up to a life.

⁂ ⁂ ⁂

What kind of life do I want for myself?
What choices will create this kind of life?

⁂ ⁂ ⁂

1.

JUST LIVE YOUR LIFE

—or—

Choose to choose

> *Understand that the right to choose your own path is a sacred privilege. Use it. Dwell in possibilities.*
> —Oprah Winfrey

Lately I've noticed that a lot of conversations about dealing with the stresses of modern life seem to conclude with someone advising that we should all stop worrying so much and trying so hard, that we should go with the flow and "just live our life." Sometimes this is good advice, as many things are beyond our control and worrying about them will not make any difference. And we can often be so focused on the future that we miss out on all there is to enjoy in the present moment. But this advice has a serious downside: "Just live your life" can lead us to turn our back on our most sacred privilege, our ability to choose our own path. In the guise of freeing us from stress and struggle, "just live your life" can actually have the sinister effect of preventing us from making the most of our life.

When the injunction to just live our life becomes a license not to choose, we end up being pulled along by *others'* choices, simply behaving the way we always have in the past, passively reacting to life rather than actively creating the life that we really want to be living. To make the most of our life, we must first of all *choose to choose*—this is the fundamental choice underlying all other choices. We must commit ourselves to the idea that there are far more possibilities than we normally see, and then to the effort that it takes to examine these possibilities and choose the one that is best for us.[1]

AT SOME POINT, ALMOST all of us have had the feeling of being trapped. We may hate working for an impossible boss who doesn't respect us, but because we need that paycheck—and this is a lousy time to be job searching—we feel we have no choice but to stay. We may be in a relationship with a partner from whom we have long felt alienated, or whom we no longer love, or who treats us badly—but we stay because we are terrified of being alone.

There are other ways of feeling trapped, as well. We may think things are actually going quite well in our life—personally and professionally—and yet have the feeling that something important is missing. We may realize that, objectively, we have a lot to be grateful for, and yet feel that this realization is not enough, because nothing seems to excite or inspire us any longer. Whether by our negative circumstances or even by our good fortune, we feel trapped and cannot see a way out.

It is at such moments—when we feel trapped—that we must *choose to choose,* that we must commit ourselves to looking for new ways to change our life—to finding within ourselves the keys that will unlock the doors of the prison we are trapped in. This is the time to recognize that while objective constraints may, at least in part, shape our life, the trap has at least something to do with our own mindset as well: Paths are almost always open to us, small or large changes we can introduce to improve our situation. Choosing to choose means searching for the paths that lead to change.

Recognize the power of choosing to choose. Sit yourself down to reflect, to analyze, to think about the possibilities that are open to you. Ask yourself some difficult questions: What do I have to do for my life to be the way I want it to be? Where do I want to go? How do I intend to get there? Write about your options, discuss your situation with those you trust. Refuse to accept "I have no choice" as an answer.

Choosing to choose is not easy. It requires not only effort but also courage. It is about being deliberate and strategic instead of just going with the flow; it is about charting unknown paths instead of resigning yourself to the road already taken; it is about being willing to struggle and fail, rather than succumbing to the comfort of the safe and the familiar. Choosing to choose does not guarantee a solution to the feeling of being trapped, or to any other difficulty that you may be facing, but it is the mind-set that increases the likelihood of finding a solution, the mind-set that is required of you if you are to realize more of your potential for success and happiness.

So what will it be? Do you just live your life and passively resign to your predicament, or do you choose to choose and actively create the kind of life that you want for yourself? That is the choice that you have at every moment, a choice that is a prerequisite for taking advantage of the choices that are ahead of you in this book, and of the many more that can help you create the life you want.

2.

OVERLOOK LIFE'S TREASURES

—or—

Be mindful of the wonder

> *Those who dwell among the beauties and mysteries of the earth are never alone or weary of life.*
>
> —Rachel Carson

What we see in the world around us is to a large extent a matter of choice. Do we take time every day to look, *really look,* at things? To find the beauty, or the humor, or the charm, or the mystery in them? When riding the bus to work, do we stare aimlessly out the window, or do we make an effort to look at the color of the sky, the shapes of the clouds? Do we look closely enough to allow ourselves to be delighted by the funny little dog trotting along the sidewalk? Or to feel sympathy, or admiration, or sadness when we watch an elderly woman walking slowly and carefully out her front door?

It is natural to be preoccupied by our own thoughts, or to be lulled into not noticing all that is around us while we do routine errands. And there is nothing wrong in daydreaming from time to time. But the more we can be mindful of what we are doing as we are doing it, the healthier and happier we will be.

Mindfulness is a choice, and it is something we can practice: When our mind wanders—whether while eating, doing the dishes, writing a report, or walking to our car—we can gently shift our focus back to the wonders that are everywhere to be found.[2]

THE BEST ADVICE THAT I can think of for becoming more mindful is to read—and reread—Helen Keller's essay "Three Days to See." Keller, who lost her sight and hearing when she was nineteen months old as a result of an illness, writes about what she would do if she were given back the use of these senses for just three days. In the essay, she recounts a conversation she had with a friend who returned from an hour-long walk in the woods. Keller asks her friend what she saw, and the friend replies, "Nothing in particular." Keller wonders how it is possible to walk through the woods and yet see nothing worthy of note:

> I who am blind can give one hint to those who see—one admonition to those who would make full use of the gift of sight: Use your eyes as if tomorrow you would be stricken blind. . . . Hear the music of voices, the song of a bird, the mighty strains of an orchestra, as if you would be stricken deaf tomorrow. Touch each object you want to touch as if tomorrow your

tactile sense would fail. Smell the perfume of flowers, taste with relish each morsel, as if tomorrow you could never smell and taste again. Make the most of every sense; glory in all the facets of pleasure and beauty which the world reveals to you.

Sometimes all we need to do is open our senses and take in the wonders of the world. Helen Keller, despite her inability to hear or see, can remind us of how privileged we are to be able to directly experience the most precious treasures that are around us and within us—sights and sounds, tastes and textures, smells and sensations.

3.

REACT IN ANGER

—or—

Take a step back

> *Anyone can become angry. That is easy. But to be angry with the right person, to the right degree, at the right time, for the right purpose, and in the right way—this is not easy.*
>
> —ARISTOTLE

CRIMES OF PASSION ARE common. We've all heard about the sudden violent outbursts of "normal" people, who lose control—who lose themselves—in the heat of the moment, and are later filled with regret. Thankfully, most of us can curb our powerful emotions, and we do not actually follow through and kill the person we *feel* like killing. And yet, most of us are guilty of minor crimes of passion. We raise our voice at our child for dawdling when he is late for school; we fire off an exasperated e-mail to a rude customer; we curse a driver who has just cut us off. Whenever we feel the heat rise, we need to take a step back, or count to ten (or a hundred). At every given moment we have a choice—to be a slave to our emotions and react, or to take a step back—a "time-in"—and exercise restraint.[3]

PSYCHOLOGIST GEORGE LOEWENSTEIN HAS conducted research on "hot" and "cold" states. A hot state is when emotions are at a high intensity and we feel a strong urge to do something or refrain from something; a cold state is when the intensity of the emotions is low and our rational mind is more dominant in the decision-making process. We think, and usually act, in very different ways depending on which state we are in. For example, research by Daniel Gilbert demonstrates that people who shop on an empty stomach will buy more than will people who shop when they are satiated. Hungry shoppers overestimate how much they could eat, as they are feeling "hot" for food.

Shopping on an empty stomach is relatively harmless; however, a decision to act when we are in a hot state can have extremely harmful consequences. Road rage is a typical example of the danger of acting in a hot state. And teenagers, of course, are more likely to practice unsafe sex when they are aroused, no matter how aware they are of the life-threatening risks involved. All of us have had times in our life when we wished we could have turned back the clock and with it erase something we did or said.

Merely labeling a situation as a hot-state situation can help a great deal in coping with it in a more rational way. The act of labeling takes us from being immersed in the situation and reacting to it, to taking a step back and observing it. Awareness of the state makes us more likely to take the necessary precautions when in a sexual encounter, or decide to take some time to cool off when in the throes of anger.

4. OBSESSIVELY REPLAY A SCENARIO

—or—

Think and act purposefully

> *Rumination inevitably backfires. It merely compounds our misery. It's a heroic attempt to solve a problem that it is just not capable of solving.*
>
> —Mark Williams

We often ruminate about a problem we face, obsessively playing and replaying the scenario in our mind. We tend to believe that rumination will help us overcome discomfort or unhappiness, but in fact replaying the scenario over and over in our mind usually makes things worse. In the words of psychologist Mark Williams and his colleagues, "Rumination is part of the problem, not part of the solution." On the other hand, purposeful thinking—whether through writing in a journal or verbalizing our thoughts—is a much better way of dealing with psychological and emotional challenges. Purposeful action—actually *doing* something that could make us feel better—is a lot more helpful than allowing chaotic and usually very negative thinking to wreak havoc on our emotions.[4]

IMAGINE THAT YOU ARE going through a difficult period at work. You cannot stop worrying about an upcoming deadline and your strained relationship with your boss. You keep replaying the last few exchanges you had with him, how he blamed you for the failure to meet an important deadline and refused to listen to the reasons why the project was late—reasons that had very little to do with you and a great deal to do with the new policies that he recently put in place. You're sure your boss thinks you are inadequate, incapable of carrying out the task at hand. This is not true, but there seems to be no way to express this without seeming defensive or paranoid. What is worse, the problems that led to the last project's being late have not been addressed, and the deadline for the next project is looming. You can't stop thinking about the situation you're in, and this leads you to a downward spiral of worry and helplessness. What is the boss going to think of you if you don't meet the deadline? What if he fires you? How would you find a new job in this economy? How would you take care of your family without a job?

Instead of focusing on the helplessness of your situation, which gets you nowhere, you could choose to engage in an activity that will help you feel better as well as perform better.

Begin by opening a new file on your computer and writing down your thoughts and feelings about the situation. Writing will help you feel better, and the clarity you reach will help you commit to taking concrete steps toward meeting the deadline despite the challenges you face. Once you've managed to do that, and your boss is reminded of both your competence and your loyalty, you are able to broach the subject of the new policies and how they are making certain aspects of your work less efficient. Now that you are out of this particular rut, you can work on finding additional ways of improving your relationship with your boss.

5.

NEGLECT YOUR POSTURE

—or—

Carry yourself with confidence and pride

A good stance and posture reflect a proper state of mind.
—Morihei Ueshiba

When we walk into a room with slumped shoulders, dragging our feet, or with our head down, we communicate lack of confidence and energy. When we enter with a natural posture, with a strong stride, shoulders open and relaxed, we send a very different—and positive—message to those around us. But crucially, the way we hold our body sends a message not only to others but also to ourselves. When we walk like someone who is confident, we actually become more confident; the physical act of sitting up straight actually boosts our motivation and increases our energy; when we shake hands firmly, we become assertive.

Assuming the posture of how we would be if we were more assertive and energized in fact boosts our confidence and invigorates us. Our behavior changes our attitude.[5]

MARVA COLLINS WAS BORN in Alabama in the 1930s. As an African-American girl growing up in the segregated South, she experienced racism and discrimination, and yet she became a highly successful and celebrated teacher, helping thousands of at-risk students succeed. How did she do it? How did she get so many students who were written off as "unteachable" to thrive? She provided her students with the gift they needed most—the belief in themselves, the confidence that they could succeed. The source of the gift she gave others was her own self-confidence, the belief that she had in herself.

Collins says, "In those days it was quite rare to be black and to be successful." She attributes her success to her parents who, despite their economic circumstances and regardless of prevailing beliefs, brought her up "with a sense of pride." In the midst of the pervading culture of discrimination and racism that can be so devastating to a person's sense of self-worth, Collins's parents taught her to be strong and to stand up for herself.

The importance of standing up for oneself was a concept that her parents took quite literally. From a very young age Collins learned that to be proud it was important to assume a proud posture, one that communicates to everyone—to yourself and others—the message that you are worthy. Collins recalls her mother often admonishing her and her sister, "Get your head up!" Today, in her seventies, Collins still walks with her head high and communicates to all those around her—as well as to herself—her self-confidence and pride. She commands respect through her posture, her voice, her eyes—and of course, her deeds.

Sit up straight. Express pride through your stride. Carry yourself in a way that communicates to the world—and to yourself—strength and confidence.

6.

RESIGN YOURSELF TO THE STATUS QUO

—or—

Make a difference

Never doubt that a small group of thoughtful, committed people can change the world. Indeed, it is the only thing that ever has.

—Margaret Mead

It's easy to feel overwhelmed by the sheer number of serious problems that our world is facing. The falling standards in education, the rise in corporate scandals, the economic crisis—not to mention wars, pollution, and terrorism. How can I, one person among so many, make a difference? How can I, with my shortcomings and insecurities, possibly bring about meaningful change? While it is true that much of what happens in the world is beyond our control as individuals, our capacity to bring about change is greater than we imagine. I *can* make a world of difference—if I *choose* to put my mind and heart to a cause, and take action.[6]

IN THE MOVIE *Pay It Forward,* a schoolteacher assigns his class the task of finding a way to bring about positive change in the world. Trevor, one of the students, decides to do three good deeds for others—three acts of random kindness—and in return ask them to do three good deeds for three other people, who will be asked in return to do the same for others, and so on. If every person who has just been helped pays this help forward to three others, then within twenty-one rounds, everyone on earth would have been helped. The movie follows Trevor and shows how his acts create a positive ripple effect that touches numerous people whom he never meets in profound and meaningful ways.

Our sense of helplessness in the face of large-scale challenges comes from the belief that our contribution would be a mere drop in the bucket. But if we can find ways to contribute that also galvanize other people—even just a few people—we can make a significant difference. In our global village, social networks expand exponentially, and what each of us does ripples across time and space.

Make a positive difference in the world. Pay forward what has been given to you, and encourage others to do the same.

7.

PROCRASTINATE

—or—

Just do it!

> *A thousand-mile journey begins with a first step.*
>
> —LAO-TZU

PROCRASTINATION—PUTTING THINGS OFF, dragging one's feet, unnecessarily postponing what can and needs to be done today—is a pervasive phenomenon. Over 70 percent of college students, for example, identify themselves as procrastinators. The temptation to put things off is understandable, but the price we pay for procrastinating is high—studies show that procrastinators have higher levels of stress, a weaker immune system, poorer sleep, and, unsurprisingly, given all of that, lower levels of happiness.

Fortunately, the research into procrastination has also identified practical ways that can help overcome the tendency to procrastinate. The single most important technique is called "the five-minute takeoff." It consists, simply, of *starting* to do the thing you have been putting off, no matter how little you feel like doing it. Procrastinators often believe that to do something one has to truly *want* to do it—to be in the right mood, to feel inspired. This is not the case. Usually, to get the job done, it is enough merely to *begin* doing it—the initial action kick-starts the process and often brings about more action.[7]

WHILE RESEARCHING PROCRASTINATION, I told Tami, my wife, about the five-minute takeoff technique and how I often use it to jump-start my writing in the morning. She was surprised to learn that I needed to apply any technique at all to get to work: "You go straight for your computer and stay there for hours at a time. You are completely absorbed."

She's right, but that does not mean that the beginning is easy. I often find myself struggling to start my work, and sometimes the first five minutes are actually quite rough—I find myself distracted, not really into it, unmotivated to put in the mental energy that is required to be productive. But once I get into it, it is usually smooth sailing.

Overcoming my inclination to procrastinate when dealing with tasks that are not the most meaningful and enjoyable, such as grading papers or doing my taxes, is of course difficult. I sometimes need to repeat the five-minute takeoff two or three times, and push myself through those initial ten or fifteen minutes by committing to "just do it."

So if you have difficulty getting yourself to exercise, just make the choice to put on your running shoes and start running; more often than not, the action will reinforce itself. If you have a project that needs to be done, don't wait for that "right moment." Choose to act, now!

This approach can serve you well on a larger scale: Commit to your vision, your dream, don't procrastinate; find ways to start moving toward the life you want to be living right now.

8.

HOLD A GRUDGE

—or—

Forgive

> *True forgiveness is not an action after the fact, it is an attitude with which you enter each moment.*
>
> —David Ridge

No one is perfect, goes the cliché, and we know this to be true, and yet we keep on punishing ourselves and others for every deviation from the perfect path. I do not believe that we can—or ought to—forgive everything. However, I know that we hold many grudges—toward ourselves and others—that we can let go of. To forgive, in Sanskrit, is to untie—when we forgive we untie an emotional knot and unclog the emotional system. We release the free flow of emotions, and are able to feel the anger, the disappointment, the fear—as well as the pain, the compassion, and the joy. Holding a grudge is like continuously pulling on the knot, and it becomes tighter; letting go of a grudge is like loosening our grip, and the knot becomes easier to untie.[8]

TWO ZEN MONKS WERE standing by a river, preparing to wade through it to the other side, when a beautiful young woman approached them. She, too, wanted to cross, but was afraid of the turbulent water. The older of the two monks offered to carry her on his back. The woman accepted his offer, and when they got to the other side she thanked him and went off on her way.

As soon as the woman was out of earshot, the younger monk turned to his companion and chastised him for his action: "You should be ashamed of yourself. We are not allowed to touch a woman's body." They continued on their way, and after a couple of hours they approached the monastery. The younger monk turned to his colleague and said that he intends to report the incident to the head of the monastery: "You did a terrible and forbidden thing." Puzzled, the older monk turned to the younger monk and asked, "What did I do that is so terrible and forbidden?"

"You carried a beautiful young woman across the river."

"Oh, that. You are right, I did. But I left her by that river, while you're still carrying her on your back."

Let go of unnecessary weight that you're carrying on your back right now. Forgive and make your journey through life lighter, calmer, and happier.

9.

TREAT THE WORK YOU DO AS A JOB

—or—

Experience your work as a calling

> *This is the true joy in life—being used for a purpose recognized by yourself as a mighty one.*
>
> —George Bernard Shaw

We spend a good part of our waking hours at work, and yet many people derive little meaning from what occupies them for several thousand hours each year. If we do not experience a sense of purpose in our work, we can choose to do one of two things (aside from resigning ourselves to being unhappy): find work that is meaningful, or find something meaningful in our work.

We don't all have the luxury of having the perfect job—the one that reflects our values, where we work only with people we like, and whose atmosphere precisely suits our temperament. But even if we do not find ourselves in that ideal setting, we have a great deal of choice as to how we experience our daily work. Whether as a CEO or a salesman, an investment banker or a community organizer, we have some control—not complete control, perhaps, but some—over what elements of our work we focus on, and consequently, on how we experience our working life. We can, for example, remind ourselves how our work is making a difference in other people's lives; we can focus on the elements that we find exciting and interesting, the meaningful interactions that we have with colleagues and customers; or we can appreciate the opportunity our work gives us to develop or expand our professional skills. If we can find no inherent value in our current occupation, we can tell ourselves that our work provides for us and for those we care about, or that it enables us to engage in meaningful activities after hours.[9]

THERE IS A STORY about a person who walked past a construction site and asked the builders what they were doing. The first builder said that he was laying bricks; the second said that he was building a wall; the third said that he was building a cathedral to the glory of God.

The research of psychologists Amy Wrzesniewski and Jane Dutton shows just how much our mind-set—what we choose to focus on—affects our experience of work. Wrzesniewski and Dutton followed a group of hospital cleaners, and found that some of the cleaners experienced their work as a job—as something they did solely for the paycheck—and described it as boring and meaningless.

But another group perceived the same work as a calling—and experienced the hours they spent at work as engaging and meaningful. This second group of hospital cleaners did things differently from the first group: They engaged in more interactions with nurses, patients, and visitors, taking it upon themselves to make everyone they came in contact with feel better. Generally, they saw their work in its broader context: They were not merely cleaning the wards and removing the trash, but were contributing to the health of patients and the smooth functioning of the hospital.

In reality, of course, both groups were carrying out similar tasks as cleaners. But those who focused on how their work made a difference and contributed to the well-being of their patients were happier than the other cleaners. Moreover, they were also happier than were many of the medical professionals in the hospital who, like the first group of cleaners, failed to find meaning in their work.

Researchers have found similar patterns among hairdressers, engineers, and restaurant employees. Those who made the choice, conscious or not, to see their work as merely a job, were less happy, were less satisfied with their life, than were their colleagues who viewed what they did as a calling. "Even in the most restricted and routine jobs," the study concluded, "employees can exert some influence on what is the essence of their work."

Many organizations today require their employees to write a job description highlighting the technical aspects of their work. This exercise reinforces the perception of work as a job. Why not, instead, highlight those elements in your work that you find meaningful, that are significant to you? In other words, why not, rather than a job description, write a *calling description*?

10.

AVOID LEARNING FROM HARDSHIP

—or—

Actively learn the lessons of hardship

> *Never let a good crisis go to waste.*
>
> —Anne Harbison

Although I do not wish hardship on myself, hardship often finds me, and when it does, I have a choice. I can treat it as a purely negative experience—one that I should put behind me as soon as possible and never think of again—or I can actively seek to identify and understand the lesson that every hardship contains within it. For example, through hardship I can learn about humbleness (gaining a better understanding of my limitations), empathy (learning to connect to the pain of others), patience (absorbing the lesson that things do not always turn out as we planned), and resilience (gaining confidence from my ability to bounce back after the hardship is overcome). I most certainly do not have to be happy about everything that is thrown my way, and yet once something negative happens to me, I can use it as a tool for development and growth. Things do not necessarily happen for the best, but I can choose to make the best of things that happen.[10]

IN THE YEAR 2000, Catalina Escobar tragically lost her son in an accident. Although devastated by her loss, she chose to take action, dedicating her life, from that point on, to saving other children. She decided to focus her efforts in the Colombian city of Cartagena, where infant mortality rates were close to fifty in a thousand (compared to five in a thousand in developed countries). Catalina founded the Juan Felipe Gómez Escobar Foundation, which provides children at risk with appropriate nutrition, and young mothers with important health counseling and services. As a result of her efforts, thousands of children's lives have been saved, and many more than that will continue to be saved in the future.

Catalina has become a champion of children's health. She speaks around the world about creating similar ventures that can make all the difference in children's lives, as well as in the lives of their parents. The organization that she built combines social services with efficient business practices, and has become a model for other poverty-stricken cities in Colombia and elsewhere.

Does Catalina think that the death of her child happened for the best? I doubt it, and I am sure that, were it possible, she would do everything that she could to bring him back. However, as a result of the tragedy she experienced, she discovered within herself remarkable strengths that gave her resilience to bounce back and bring about significant change in herself and, by extension, in her community.

Find the lessons in difficulties that you are facing right now. Look back and learn from hardships that you've experienced in the past; you will not only derive important lessons from reflecting on these challenges, you will also realize how much you have grown as a result.

11.

ALLOW OTHERS TO UPSET YOU

—or—

Appreciate and learn from those around you

> *Appreciation is to humans what the sun is for plants.*
>
> —Frank Iversen

There are certain people—ones we know intimately and others we meet for the first time—who, for one reason or another, irritate us. It could be the way they act or talk, the way they look or walk. And while there is no need to always change our perspective about those people—leaving the scene or minimizing the time we spend with them could be the right thing to do—we lose many opportunities when we mindlessly succumb to the dictates of our unpleasant reactions.

Reflecting on the source of our dislike toward another person can reveal something about ourselves, because we often get annoyed by precisely those things we dislike in ourselves. Learning to appreciate things about the person who vexes us can help us cultivate the *benefit-finder* within, as well as develop deeper compassion—both of which will contribute to our relationships with others and with ourselves.[11]

LOVING KINDNESS MEDITATIONS HAVE been practiced for thousands of years in the East. More recently, Western scientists have demonstrated the remarkable benefits of this practice. The basic idea behind this form of meditation is simple—directing kindness, generosity, benevolence, or positive emotions in general toward ourselves and toward others.

We begin with the "easy" low-hanging fruits for feeling kindness, and then expand the circle of kindness to include other people about whom we may not feel as positively. For example, I may start with thinking about my child and experiencing loving kindness toward him, and then once I experience that emotion, I can think of someone else who may not be as close to me and direct my positive feelings toward him as well. In this way, I can expand my circle of loving kindness to others about whom I may have ambivalent feelings.

I remember doing this exercise in one of my two-day workshops, where the first day didn't go well at all. A number of the participants were cynical about positive psychology, and I became increasingly restless during the course of the day. The second day, I woke up and did loving kindness meditation, directing my love first toward the members of my family, one by one, and then expanding it toward participants in the workshop. I really felt genuine kindness and love toward the participants when I meditated. Later on I arrived at the workshop, brimming with positive emotions. The second day of the workshop went extremely well and I learned a great deal, especially from the skeptical participants. Whether this was because of the meditation, I don't know—there was no control group for me to test this on—but even if my mini-intervention did not have any effect on the quality of my teaching, it had a significant effect on the quality of my experience.

Is there a particular person who upsets you? Is it a particular trait or behavior? Try loving kindness meditation, and experience positive emotions toward that person.

12.

IMPRESS AND CONCEAL

—or—

Express and reveal

> *Vulnerability is the core of shame and fear and our struggle for worthiness, but it appears that it's also the birthplace of joy, of creativity, of belonging, of love.*
>
> —Brené Brown

To express myself—to openly share my thoughts and feelings—is to risk being rejected and hurt by others. But choosing *not* to express myself and to hide behind a facade, no matter how impressive that facade is, is a form of self-rejection that leads to unhappiness and discontent. While it is the case that if I am true to myself others *may* not like what they see, it is *certain* that if I constantly put on a show, eventually I will not like myself.

Putting on a facade is often an indicator of low self-esteem. But far from being a fix for the problem, pretending to be someone I am not has the effect, over time, of *lowering* my self-esteem. Moreover, even if others like what they see when I put on a show, it is not me that they like, but the person I am pretending to be. When I choose the real over the unreal, the authentic over the inauthentic—when I express rather than impress—I no longer apologize for who I am. I allow my inner light to shine.[12]

PROFESSOR BRENÉ BROWN STUDIED people who enjoy a high self-esteem. Her objective was to understand what it was about them that was different from people who feel unworthy. The one distinguishing characteristic that she identified was courage—courage to be imperfect and to be vulnerable.

Rather than constantly being concerned about whether their love would be reciprocated, they gave love first. Rather than choosing not to apply for a position they really wanted but had little chance of getting, they plunged in. Rather than concerning themselves about how they would be perceived, they were authentic—"willing to let go of who they thought they should be in order to be who they were." Rather than hide their vulnerabilities and imperfections, they shared them.

Allowing ourselves to be vulnerable, to let go of the mask of perfection, is very hard. Vulnerability comes at a price—it can hurt a lot! But this cost is negligible compared to the cost we pay when we suppress part of our humanity. When we do not allow ourselves to be vulnerable, we are also suppressing our joy and happiness and the potential to cultivate deep and meaningful connections in our life.

Can you open up a little more, reveal part of your true self? Go on, be vulnerable, be real!

13. FOCUS ON DEFEATING THE OTHER

—or—

Seek the win-win

There's plenty out there and enough to spare for everybody. An Abundance Mentality involves sharing prestige, recognition, profits, and decision making. It opens possibilities, options, alternatives, and creativity.

—STEPHEN R. COVEY

IN MOST DISPUTES—WHETHER a minor domestic spat or a major political conflict—it is possible to find a solution that benefits both sides. When I set out to fight and defeat my opponent, I end up expending a great deal of energy on destroying rather than on creating the maximum value. Moreover, entering a dispute with a win-lose approach often leads to a similar approach being adopted by the other party. As a result, both of us may end up losing.

When I show goodwill and a desire to help, I invite similar behavior from the other. When we put our joint resources, our mind and heart, to the task of increasing the benefits to the individual and the group, we stand a better chance of success—for all who are involved. The pleasure of winning when the other side loses is short-lived; the joy of a win-win outcome lasts a great deal longer, and often creates the basis for yet another round of positive experiences.[13]

IN A STUDY CONDUCTED at Stanford University, Lee Ross and Steven Samuels asked students to nominate their most cooperative and most competitive classmates. Those nominated, not knowing that they were selected for their particular characteristics, were then asked to participate in a prisoners' dilemma game—a game in which each participant can choose a win-win cooperative approach or a win-lose competitive approach. Through a random assignment, half the students were told that the exercise was called the Community Game, and the other half that it was the Wall Street Game.

The majority of those who were in the Community Game cooperated, whereas the majority of those who were in the Wall Street Game did not. Whether participants were nominated for being competitive or cooperative was a very weak predictor of their behavior in the game. What made the difference was the context in which the situation was framed.

We, too, have control over how we frame the context in which we act—both with respect to particular situations and to life as a whole. If we approach a situation with the intention of making it win-win (just as participants in the Community Game did), we are a great deal more likely to cooperate and find an outcome that will indeed make all involved better off. Our relationships will improve a great deal, and we will enjoy life a lot more, if we seek the win-win outcome.

The next time you interact with someone, whether the context is a cooperative or a competitive one, think about how you can both benefit, how you can both win.

14.

RUSH THROUGH LIFE

—or—

Savor life

> *The golden moments in the stream of life rush past us and we see nothing but sand; the angels come to visit us, and we only know them when they are gone.*
>
> —George Eliot

The guiding axiom of modern life is that more is better. But we pay a heavy price for placing quantity above quality. Activities, no matter how potentially enjoyable they are, bring us no pleasure if we are constantly on the run, racing from one thing to the next. Even the most delicious food in the world can give me no enjoyment if I devour it as fast as I can. To be a wine connoisseur, I cannot chug the entire glass in one gulp; to fully enjoy the richness of the drink, I smell, I taste, I savor, I take my time. To become a connoisseur of life, to enjoy the richness that life has to offer, I sometimes need to slow down, to take my time.[14]

ERIC BRUN-SANGLARD IS THE Blind Designer. He guides his clients through the process of creating a home that does not just look right, but that feels right. His personal story can teach us to savor our life, to be more in touch with what the outer and inner worlds have to offer.

Eric was in his thirties when he lost his sight. Until then, he was a highly successful businessman, jet-setting around the world, working as a creative director for such companies as Christian Dior, Hermès, and Chanel. And then, illness struck, and Eric became blind. He was forced to stop, to slow down, and to reevaluate his life. At that time he was designing his own home in Los Angeles, and rather than delegate the rest of the project to someone else who could see, he decided to complete the work himself. The experience led him to start his own design business, which is thriving.

When Eric meets prospective clients, he listens to their words and to the messages beyond the words; by slowing down he is able to sense their wants and connect to their needs. And he does the same when walking into a space, slowing down and feeling a room, listening to the natural sounds inside and outside, sensing what the house needs to become a home.

Eric's blindness taught him that the first step to truly see the potential of a room, the richness in the world, or the beauty in our life, is to slow down.

Can you slow down just a little and, rather than rush through life, savor its treasures and gifts?

15.

EAT MINDLESSLY

—or—

Treat your body with respect

> *Nutrition has a profound impact on practically all the leading causes of disease in Western societies.*
>
> —David Servan-Schreiber

While people in many parts of the world are suffering from malnutrition, others, especially in the West, are suffering from overnutrition. To those of us in the latter group, not only is food accessible and cheap, its taste is artificially enhanced. The result is that at almost every moment of our life, we are enticed to choose food that is bad for us. Given that we consume more than we should, and that much of what we eat is unhealthy, it is no wonder that obesity is on the rise, as are related chronic ailments such as diabetes, cancer, and heart disease. To lead a longer, healthier, and better life, we have to be more mindful about the quantity and quality of the foods we ingest.[15]

"BLUE ZONES" IS THE term used to identify those places around the world where people live longer and better—places where there are more centenarians than anywhere else, and where more people not only live longer but also remain fully functioning well into their eighties and nineties. Building on the work carried out by researchers such as Dr. Robert Kane from the National Institute of Aging, Dan Buettner and his team from *National Geographic* studied the Blue Zones with the goal of "discovering the world's best practices in health and longevity and putting them to work in our lives."

Not surprisingly, Buettner discovered that healthy eating ranks high on the list of practices that distinguish residents of the Blue Zones. And there are no great surprises when it comes to nutrition: natural rather than processed foods; an abundance of fruits, vegetables, and nuts; and so on.

But it's not just the quality of food that matters, it's also the quantity. In Okinawa, the locals say to themselves before a meal, "Eat until you are 80 percent full." This message, repeated daily, makes them mindful not to overeat. Buettner notes that in the West we typically stop eating when we're full, whereas in Okinawa they stop when they're no longer hungry.

In general, the eating habits of those living in the Blue Zones are characterized by moderation. The people there do not go to the extreme of starving themselves, nor do they deprive themselves entirely of all unhealthy food pleasures. At the same time, they do not overindulge as so many of us do. Our body is capable of disposing of unhealthy ingredients present in some foods, but cannot keep up with the excessive intake of the toxins that are present in most modern diets.

I personally have adopted the Okinawan practice of eating in moderation. It took me a few months to change my eating habits, and during that time I wore a wristband to remind myself of the "80 percent full" rule and, more generally, to be more mindful of what and how I eat.

Treat your body with respect. Enjoy your food, enjoy abundance, but in moderation—so that you can continue to enjoy it all for many years to come.

16.

OVERLOOK CHANCE OPPORTUNITIES

—or—

Create your own luck

> *The truth knocks on the door and you say, "Go away, I'm looking for the truth" and so it goes away.*
>
> —Robert M. Pirsig

Opportunities so often knock on our door—in the form of a coincidence, a chance encounter, an unexpected gift, a surprise—and we don't pay attention to them. We dismiss them and go on with our life as if nothing important happened. And indeed, if this is what we choose to believe, then nothing of significance *has* happened or will happen. We owe it to ourselves to seize those opportunities and make the most of what comes our way. Whether or not we believe in divine providence, whether or not we believe that apparently random experiences contain meaningful lessons that are directly relevant to our life, there is much to be gained from paying attention to chance occurrences, to what psychologist Carl Jung called *synchronicity*.[16]

CLEARLY THERE ARE ASPECTS of life over which we have no control. But the extent to which we *do* have the capacity to create our own luck is substantial. Richard Wiseman of the University of Hertfordshire studied lucky people, both those who considered themselves lucky and those whom others considered lucky. In his research, he found that there were actual characteristics—behavioral and thought patterns—that distinguish the lucky from the unlucky.

One of the ways that people who are considered lucky actually create their luck is by noticing and capitalizing on chance encounters. Where most people see a meaningless coincidence, lucky people see a meaningful opportunity. Lucky people don't wait for luck to come their way; they actually create it by changing their usual routines: the newspapers they read, the route they take to work, the activities they attend, the people they choose to approach. These changes increase the likelihood that they'll encounter meaningful opportunities.

Another characteristic of lucky people is that they tend to focus on the full part of the glass. If, for example, they're robbed, they express gratitude for not being physically hurt; if they underperform on a task, they tend to think about what they have learned from the experience and how they can grow. In this way, through their interpretation of an event, they transform something that others would consider a negative (being robbed, underperforming) into a positive (not being hurt, an opportunity to learn). This interpretation about something that happened *in the past* affects what will happen *in the future.* Beliefs often act as self-fulfilling prophecies, and those who believe that they are lucky are much more likely to be so in real life.

Start to create your own luck by changing your routine, by doing things differently, and by noticing how lucky you already are.

17.

ENGAGE IN NEGATIVE SELF-TALK

—or—

Remind yourself of your true self

> *Habits of thinking need not be forever. One of the most significant findings in psychology in the last twenty years is that individuals can choose the way they think.*
>
> —Martin Seligman

Inside our head we have a continuous stream of thoughts, many of which contain negative messages that harm us. And because we have been living with these messages for so long, we confuse them with reality and act as if they were true. For example, many people believe that they do not deserve to be happy, or to be loved, or to succeed. Other people believe they cannot learn math or master certain skills. More often than not, these negative messages are baseless and irrational. We listen to them and accept them unthinkingly as true simply because we have heard them inside our mind for so long.

Instead of allowing these messages to replay endlessly in your mind unchallenged, step up and raise your rational voice to contest them one by one. Take back control over the messages that you listen to and live by.[17]

PROFESSOR JEFFREY SCHWARTZ AND his colleagues at UCLA have created an intervention program that can help people banish negative messages from their mind. Through the program, people realize that many of the messages that they have internalized and accepted unthinkingly at face value were actually implanted in their mind by others (for instance, by significant adults or the media). Once they are able to recognize these messages for what they are—internalizations of the subjective ideas of others, rather than their own true beliefs about themselves—they can begin to free themselves from the oppressive and harmful consequences of these negative messages.

Schwartz gives the example of Sarah, who internalized the message that in order to be loved and accepted she had to be perfect as well as put everyone else's needs before her own. While this message was clearly distorted and false, for Sarah it was reality. It led Sarah to obsess over each word and gesture that her friends and colleagues made. And as it was a standard that neither she nor anyone else could possibly live up to, she perceived herself as a loser, feeling depressed and worthless. She became physically and psychologically ill: She lost all motivation to go out and meet people, to exercise, to be part of the world.

It was only after she recognized that this image of herself that she had was not true—that is, was a "deceptive brain message"—that Sarah got her life back. Her recovery did not happen overnight: It took a great deal of work to change the habits of thought that had been cultivated over many years. But once Sarah identified the negative thoughts for what they really were, they lost their power over her.

We may not always have a choice about whether we get to hear these negative internal messages—we may, for instance, simply be too young to resist—but we *do* have a choice about what to do with them *now.*

Do you choose to surrender to these oppressive messages and live your life in accordance with their dictates, or do you choose to reject them and live a life that is true to your real self?

18.

OVERLOOK THE GOOD IN OTHERS

—or—

Commend and compliment

> *I can live for two months on a good compliment.*
>
> —Mark Twain

Compliments are not just throwaway phrases that are pleasant to receive. If we fail to appreciate the positive in other people, the positive will depreciate and we'll have less of it. Each time I go out of my way to commend and compliment my partner, my child, my employee, or myself, I am strengthening and empowering both those I am complimenting and my relationship with them. Just as depositing money in a savings account when things are going well helps to weather financial difficulties, offering positive feedback on a regular basis helps a relationship weather hard times. It costs us nothing to dispense smiles and warm words, at home or in the workplace, and the benefit that we get in the ultimate currency of happiness is priceless.[18]

IN THEIR CHILDREN'S BOOK *Have You Filled a Bucket Today?*, Carol McCloud and David Messing describe a world in which each of us metaphorically carries around an invisible bucket. The purpose of the bucket is to hold our positive thoughts and feelings about ourselves: We feel good when our bucket is full, and we are unhappy when it is empty.

When we make others feel good—by complimenting, by being kind, or simply by smiling—we help them fill up their bucket. When we make them feel bad—by putting them down, by ridiculing them, by hurting them in some way—we drain their bucket of the positive emotions that it contained. The beauty of the good deed and the kind word is that by helping others fill their bucket we simultaneously fill our own. To give is to receive.

This parable, though for children, is an important reminder for us all. You can begin to look at yourself—in your role as a lawyer, teacher, banker, pharmacist, friend, partner, or parent—as a bucket filler. By your being a bucket filler, your life and the life of those around you will instantly become so much better.

19.

GO THROUGH LIFE AS A FAULT-FINDER

—or—

Be a benefit-finder

> *Make a game of finding something positive in every situation. Ninety-five percent of your emotions are determined by how you interpret events to yourself.*
>
> —Brian Tracy

According to Henry David Thoreau, "The fault-finder will find faults even in paradise." The fault-finder is constantly on the lookout for problems and flaws in people and situations. Seeking faults, he finds them, of course—even in paradise. The alternative approach to life is captured by the benefit-finder, who finds the silver lining in the dark cloud, who makes lemonade out of lemons, who looks on the bright side of life, and who does not fault writers for using too many clichés! We can look for the good in every situation and in every person. And in most cases—not all, but most—we will find the good. How we choose to approach life—whether as a benefit-finder or a fault-finder—significantly impacts our physical and mental health, our experience of the world, and the experiences of those around us.[19]

I WANT TO SHARE with you a few personal stories.

I have attention deficit disorder. My mind wanders constantly, and I find it difficult to focus for any length of time on one activity. At times, my ADD makes learning and working incredibly difficult.

Since the age of eleven, I dreamed of being a professional squash player. When I was twenty, just as I was getting ready to embark on a professional career in my sport of choice, I was injured. The injury was devastating emotionally. It shattered my dream.

I was kicked out of the PhD program at Cambridge University in England—the only student in my year (and one of the few ever) to be expelled. All in all, it was a humiliating experience and a wasted year, professionally and academically.

I am so unlucky!

Now let me tell you the same facts, seen a bit differently.

I have attention deficit disorder. It's actually a good thing, because it forces me to focus on those activities that I actually love, because only something I am passionate about can capture my attention. It is a blessing: an internal mechanism that forces me to do things that make me happy.

Since the age of eleven, I dreamed of being a professional squash player. When I was twenty, just as I was getting ready to pursue my dream, I was injured. The injury ended my professional aspirations. As a result I decided to apply to university, and discovered psychology, which has been my passion ever since.

I was kicked out of the PhD program at Cambridge University—the only student in my year (and one of the few ever) to be expelled. This experience turned out to be a blessing in disguise, preparing me for my future work as a consultant. I was at the time arrogant and full of myself—a likely prescription for failure. Being kicked out of the program humbled me, and I ended up spending some of the best years of my life living and working in Asia.

I am so lucky!

Same events, different interpretation—first as a fault-finder, and then as a benefit-finder. Now, it's not that having ADD or giving up a dream or being thrown out of a program is easy and fun. However, looking at events through the lens of a benefit-finder can help us perceive and experience the world in a different—often better—way.

Describe a few events in your life, first by focusing on the negatives, and then by highlighting the upside of these same experiences. Can you live your life as a benefit-finder?

20.

RUSH TO GIVE ADVICE

—or—

Listen with empathy and openness

It is the province of knowledge to speak, and it is the privilege of wisdom to listen.

—Oliver Wendell Holmes

The key to providing emotional and moral support to people in need, is the ability to listen to what they are saying. When others need our help, our instinct is to rush in and provide comfort and practical advice. But no matter how valuable the knowledge that we wish to share, no matter how well intentioned our desire to help, our first obligation is to provide the space and the opportunity for others to share experiences, feelings, and thoughts. We need to curb our inclination to think about our response while others are speaking, jump to complete their sentences, or interject with our advice—even if it is the best advice possible.

Learning from the experience and advice of others is extremely important—it is one of principal ways in which we grow as individuals. But it usually works only if those receiving the advice feel that they have been heard.[20]

PERHAPS THE MOST COMMON characteristic associated with great leadership is charisma—the ability to excite others by delivering rousing speeches or conveying an inspiring message. It turns out, though, that charisma is overrated and that a more important characteristic of great leaders is their ability to listen.

In the early 1970s, Robert Greenleaf coined the term *servant leadership* after noticing that the great leaders throughout history spoke and acted as servants. Biblical leaders such as Moses and Jesus were depicted as servants, as were more recent political leaders such as Mahatma Gandhi and Martin Luther King. After spending twenty-seven years in prison, Nelson Mandela's words to the people of South Africa were, "I am your servant." Great business leaders such as Jim Burke of Johnson & Johnson and Anita Roddick of the Body Shop believed that their primary responsibility as a CEO was to serve and be attentive to the needs of their employees and customers.

According to Greenleaf and other leadership scholars, one of the core characteristics of servant leaders is that they listen first and talk later. In fact, to become a servant leader, Greenleaf argued, a person has to go through "a long arduous discipline of learning to listen, a discipline sufficiently sustained that the automatic response to any problem is to listen first."

We are all leaders, at least in some situations and some of the time: at home, at work, in our community center, when we're with friends or family or colleagues. When others share with us something important, they are looking up to us for help, for leadership. And if we want to be effective leaders and help them, we first need to learn how to listen.

21.

CHASE THE NEXT MATERIAL ACQUISITION

—or—

Invest in experiences

> *It is not how much we have, but how much we enjoy,*
> *that makes happiness.*
> —Charles Spurgeon

Many people believe that the secret to happiness lies in having the bigger home, the faster car, the newer gadget, the fatter bank account. The advertising industry, by and large, inspires and boosts material worship, promising eternal bliss right after the next acquisition. As it turns out, though, once our basic needs are met, acquiring more possessions—bigger, better, newer, shinier—doesn't make us any happier. At most, it gives us a temporary high, similar to addicts' getting their fix.

Lasting happiness comes not from possessing material things but from pursuing positive experiences—playing ball with your child, enjoying a meal with a friend, tasting the salt in the air as you walk by the sea. I can afford these experiences; I cannot afford to live without them. Their price tag is low, and yet they are priceless.[21]

YOU HAVE JUST RECEIVED your year-end bonus, which was significantly higher than you expected. You worked extremely hard during the year, and you feel that you deserve a reward. And here is the dilemma you face: Do you spend the money on a newer, better car, or do you take your family on a vacation? You figure that a vacation would be nice, but it will be over before you know it, whereas a car will last for years. So you decide to get the car.

It turns out that your reasoning is wrong. Research by marketing professor Leonardo Nicolao and his colleagues shows that once our basic needs have been met, we typically derive greater long-term happiness from acquiring *experiences* than from acquiring *goods.* Although the experience may be short-lived and the material good remains with us for much longer, we continue to enjoy the experience—to reexperience it—through our memories and conversations, whereas the novelty of a new object wears off very quickly.

The picture is a bit different if the material good provides us pleasant experiences. If, for example, I enjoy fixing cars, or racing them, then a car can provide me with many positive experiences. Nevertheless, here, too, the criterion by which I ought to evaluate a purchase is the type of experience that I will get.

It is not only when we enjoy a windfall (such as a year-end bonus) that we ought to think about the value of experiences. Our lesser, day-to-day decisions can also be informed by recognizing the advantage of experiences over goods, leading us to prefer an evening at the theater or going bowling with the family over a new gadget or toy.

22.

BE DEFENSIVE

—or—

Be open to suggestions

> *We say we want the truth; what we mean is that we want to be correct.*
>
> —Mihnea Moldoveanu

One of the defining characteristics of perfectionists is their defensiveness in the face of criticism. Why? Because a criticism points out an imperfection, a flaw, and this is something that a perfectionist finds difficult to accept. Many people, not just perfectionists, find it difficult to truly be open and magnanimous when criticized. The price we pay for being defensive is extremely high, because dogmatically rejecting criticism is putting up a wall between us and potentially useful ideas, as well as between us and other people. We deprive ourselves of real growth as well as real intimacy.[22]

MY NAME IS TAL and I am a perfectionist.

According to psychologist Karen Horney, perfectionism—being a form of neurosis—never entirely goes away. However, while there are always remnants of a neurosis, it can potentially weaken over time and have less of a hold on us. Over the years, I have become less of a perfectionist, much of it thanks to the work I did—and am doing—around being less defensive.

When I realized and acknowledged that I was defensive—and realized the price I was paying for attacking and dismissing any and all unfavorable judgments—I decided to change. My approach was behavioral in nature. Specifically, I would solicit criticism from others—whether about my writing or my way of managing—and when the person obliged me I would hold myself back from responding. Initially, refraining from launching a harsh and dismissive diatribe was difficult, but over time it has become easier—not easy, but easier—for me to accept feedback.

Over the years, as I became more open and generous in my reaction to criticism, my personal and professional life improved significantly.

Make a point of soliciting feedback, of asking others where you can improve. And when you receive feedback, be open, really listen, and learn.

23.

REFRAIN FROM SAYING NO

—or—

Say yes only when your vision is served

> *A no uttered from the deepest conviction is better than a yes merely uttered to please, or worse, to avoid trouble.*
>
> —Mahatma Gandhi

No is one of the shortest words in the English language, and one of the easiest to pronounce—and yet it is one of the most difficult words for so many of us to utter. We often end up saying yes because we want to please, because we don't want to let others down, or because we fear that their disappointment will turn to anger, which will be directed toward us. We forget, however, that sometimes saying yes to others is tantamount to saying no to ourselves. To become happier and more successful, we have to focus our sights on our own vision. This implies learning to say no more often—to people as well as opportunities—which is not easy. It means prioritizing, choosing activities that we really want to be involved in, while letting go of others.[23]

SAYING NO IS DIFFICULT for me. A while back, during a very busy period in my life, I started to feel nauseous and light-headed, for no apparent reason. I was traveling for work at the time, so I made an appointment to see my doctor when I returned home. During those few days between making the appointment and seeing my doctor, part of me hoped that she would find some stress-related problem and order me to cut down on work. I then imagined calling a few people with whom I was working on various projects, and telling them that I have to stop on doctor's orders.

It took me a couple of days to realize the meaning of this fantasy scenario that I had been playing in my head. There were certain projects that I really did not want to be involved in, and yet I participated in them (even though I could drop out of them if I wanted to) simply because I was unable to say no. I was even willing to pay a high price (in terms of my physical health) if this meant that I could get someone else to say no on my behalf. As soon as I realized this, I was able to find the courage to listen to myself and follow my own desires. I called up the persons involved, and with as much empathy as I could muster, opted out of the projects.

Are there projects or activities that you would be better off without? What can you say no to?

24.

REFUSE TO ACCEPT REALITY

—or—

Accept reality and act on it

> *Face reality as it is, not as it was or as you wish it to be.*
>
> —Jack Welch

While we can change certain things, other things are out of our control. And if something is really out of our control, we have to learn to accept it regardless of how much we wish it were different. We may not like the law of gravity and may wish it did not exist, and yet most of us accept it and learn to live with it. If we refuse to accept the reality of this law, we will not survive for long, and even if we do, we will experience constant frustration. The same applies to every fact of reality, such as the fact that it is impossible to literally go back in time and undo something that was done, or the fact that all of us have some real physical limitations.

Instead of evading reality and spending our life engaged in wishful thinking, we ought to spend our time and effort on real thinking.[24]

SOCIOLOGIST AARON ANTONOVSKY, WIDELY considered one of the founders of the science of well-being, argues that suffering is inherent to human existence. Some twenty-five hundred years ago, the Buddha proposed suffering as the first noble truth. According to Antonovsky and the Buddha, difficulties, dissatisfaction, despair, and unhappiness are part and parcel of every life. Are they both fundamentally pessimistic about human life? No, they're realistic!

This realism comes in stark contrast to the promises dispensed by some self-help gurus today who claim to know the shortcut to the good life: They promise five easy steps to success, or three keys to fame and fortune, or the one secret to living happily ever after. But the truth is that there are no shortcuts, no getting around the real work—the daily effort and struggle—that is required for living a full and fulfilling life.

After recognizing the reality of suffering, Antonovsky went on to study how some people learn to better deal with suffering, whereas the Buddha explored how to relieve suffering. Both of them generated some of the most profound and influential ideas for leading a better life.

Whether your concern is business, science, relationships, or leading a happier life, success requires that you first face reality.

25.

TREAT LIFE WITH GRAVITY

—or—

Bring humor and lightness

> *A person without a sense of humor is like a wagon without springs. It's jolted by every pebble on the road.*
>
> —Henry Ward Beecher

Psychologists use the term *cognitive reconstruction* to describe our ability to look at a situation from different perspectives. In difficult times and in tough situations it can be beneficial for us to look at things from a new angle, including seeing the humorous element—the lighter and brighter side—of our troubles. Of course, there are times when solemnity and gravity are the appropriate response, but more often than not we take ourselves—and life—too seriously, and we miss out on the comical and the playful. Regaining that spark of laughter and fun that we may have lost after childhood will make life more pleasant, contribute to our psychological and physical health, and will, of course, make us more pleasant to be around.[25]

NORMAN COUSINS WAS IN his late forties when he was diagnosed with severe arthritis. He needed painkillers to get through the day, and sleeping pills to sleep at night. And his doctors told him that his days were numbered.

Cousins remembered reading somewhere that stress and painful emotions might negatively affect the immune system. At the time, this was merely a hypothesis, but Cousins was convinced that it was true. Armed with his conviction, he decided to do battle with his disease. He left the hospital and began his own self-prescribed alternative treatment whose main component was laughter. He watched Marx Brothers movies and hired a nurse to read him funny stories. He soon discovered that after enjoying a dose of belly laughter, he was free of pain for a couple of hours. Eventually, the treatment was so successful that he was completely off sleeping pills and painkillers and returned to work.

It took the scientific community years to catch up with Cousins's findings. Today you can find countless studies that illustrate how laughter can alleviate pain and strengthen the immune system. Through the tireless work of Patch Adams, the medical clown, and many others around the world, humor has been embraced as an important component of the healing process.

You don't need the excuse of illness to bring more humor to your life and enjoy higher levels of happiness, better relationships, and improved health. Introduce levity into your days: Watch a favorite TV program, read jokes on the Internet, or meet up with a friend who makes you laugh.

26.

BE PART OF THE RAT RACE

—or—

Focus on what truly matters

> *Society tells us the only thing that matters is matter—the only things that count are the things that can be counted.*
>
> —Laurence G. Boldt

We often measure the value of our life by what we think are "objective" criteria—our class ranking, the money we earn, the number of trophies we have won, the cars parked in our garage—or by the amount of "things" we get done. In fact, however, research has repeatedly shown that success measured by these standards does not lead to long-lasting happiness. At most, it provides a temporary increase in well-being.

More is not always better. The path to finding emotional fulfillment and long-term happiness requires us to identify and focus on the things that truly matter to us, whatever they may be, regardless of what our culture tells us that we should want to be or to do. This could mean getting involved in work-related projects that are emotionally satisfying to us, or it could mean making sure that we spend time with the people we care about and who care about us.[26]

IN THE MOVIE *CLICK*, the main character Michael Newman lives life in the fast lane. His primary focus is on getting promoted at work—the one thing he believes will truly make him happy. One day, Michael receives a magic remote control device that enables him to fast-forward his life and he uses it to skip past everything that happens on the road to his promotion. He fast-forwards through hard work and hard times, but also through all the daily pleasures of life—including making love to his wife—because all of these slow his progress to his ultimate goal. He considers everything that is not directly related to his end goal an unnecessary detour.

To those around him, Michael seems fully awake, but the effect of using the remote control is that Michael is sedated—not for a few hours to avoid the pain of an operation, but for most of his life—so that he can avoid experiencing the journey, which he perceives as an impediment to his happiness. Michael essentially sleeps through life, not actually being there for all those activities that are not directly related to his career goals and aspirations. It is only when Michael is an old man that he realizes the gravity of his mistake—that he essentially skipped over all those precious moments that make life worth living.

Of course, this being a Hollywood movie, Michael gets a second chance, and this time around he does not make the same mistake: He chooses to experience his life rather than fast-forward through it, and he is a much happier and better person as a result. In real life, of course, people who solely focus on their long-term goals and miss everything that matters in the here and now, get no second chance.

What matters most to you? Why not spend more time pursuing those activities that are personally meaningful to you? Why not dedicate yourself to those things in life that truly count?

27.

AVOID THE EFFORT OF THINKING

—or—

Focus and think

> *The question "to be or not to be" is the question "to think or not to think."*
>
> —Ayn Rand

According to Aristotle, what distinguishes us from other animals is our rationality—our ability to think. To assert our humanity we have to think and reason, which at times requires effort. Other animals are born with instincts that guide and lead them to preserving their life. The instincts we have as human beings are insufficient for surviving, let alone for thriving. An animal, for example, does not ask itself, "What is my purpose?" or "How should I spend the next day, week, or ten years of my life?" or "What kind of education should I give my children?"

To be the author of my life, my action has to be a product of my thinking, not my ability to circumvent the process of thinking. To lead a full and fulfilling life I cannot afford to rely on my instincts, or to outsource thinking to other people. I have to think.[27]

I MET RON AT a seminar for educators who work with at-risk groups. He was one of the speakers, and on the final day of the seminar he recounted his personal journey.

Ron had a criminal record at fourteen, and by the time he was fifteen he had stopped counting how many nights he had spent in jail. Just short of his seventeenth birthday he was sent to a boarding school for teens with a criminal record, where he met a teacher who changed his life. Ron said that his teacher did most of the right things that had been discussed during the first two days of the seminar: He cared about him and believed in him and listened to him and genuinely wanted him to succeed. "But the most important thing he did for me," said Ron, "was that he got me to think."

Ron paused for a few seconds, overcome by emotion. "He said to me, 'No one can think for you, and whether you waste your life or make something of it depends on whether you think about what you want to do and about the consequences of your actions.' I heard him, and my life changed."

Today, Ron runs a small business, and spends some of his free time spreading his teacher's message to children in trouble with the law. "It's the most important message they need to hear," he says, and then, smiling, he adds, "I think."

28.

WORRY

—*or*—

Move on

Worry never robs tomorrow of its sorrow, it only saps today of its joy.

—LEO BUSCAGLIA

WORRYING CAN SERVE AN important purpose: If we worry about something today, we can take action to avert trouble in the future. Most of the time, however, we worry about what is beyond our control, or about things that are trivial and unimportant. Whenever I worry, I remind myself to step back and ask myself whether my worry serves a purpose. If it does, then I should take action! If, however, it does not, then I need to label my preoccupation as unnecessary worry, and move on to other more useful pursuits.

Although it may be difficult initially to shift my focus away from worry, I know that over time I will gain better control over what preoccupies me and learn to move on when I engage in futile concern.[28]

STANFORD PSYCHIATRIST IRVIN YALOM studied terminally ill patients. When patients are told there is no hope, the news often leads to a radical shift in perspective: They cease to focus on small problems and petty worries, and they start to "trivialize the trivial" and live fully.

A related research finding is that, on average, happiness increases with age. Unlike the young, who are often consumed by unimportant issues, older people are better able to rise above the immediate and recognize what truly matters.

One of my pet worries is that my children do not eat enough. My grandmother, who is turning ninety this year, tells me that when she had my father, she, too, was concerned, and that he turned out fine. In fact, she says, that once she stopped worrying so much (following the advice of her mother), things quickly got a lot better. I'm working on it!

Life is short. The question for all of us, young and old, is how long it is going to take us to realize this. Whether we like it or not, the clock is ticking and our time here is limited. Much in the world is worth doing and worth contemplating; it would be such a shame to waste time and effort on futile concerns.

For whom the clock ticks, it ticks for thee—as a reminder of what truly matters. Make the most of the time you have!

29.

BE A PESSIMIST

—or—

Be hopeful and optimistic

> *You see things; and you say, "Why?" But I dream things that never were; and I say, "Why not?"*
>
> —George Bernard Shaw

Pessimists dismiss optimism as ungrounded and unrealistic. And while it is true that optimists, by definition, have high hopes and lofty dreams, these hopes and dreams can become self-fulfilling prophecies: Over time they can become real. A pessimistic outlook makes it more likely that the future will turn out gloomy; a hopeful disposition is likely to bring about success and well-being. If optimism and hope are grounded, they can improve the quality of our relationships, bring about success at work, help us overcome adversity, and provide an important foundation for making our dreams come true. To a great extent, my expectations of myself or others, and of situations, determine my reality.[29]

UNTIL 1954, RUNNING THE mile in under four minutes was considered a physical impossibility. Doctors and scientists all agreed that the four-minute mark represented the physiological limit of human ability. The best runners in the world confirmed the experts' view by closing in on the four-minute mile but never bettering it. Runners spoke of the "brick wall," an impenetrable barrier that existed at the four-minute mark.

Despite the prevailing conventional wisdom, Roger Bannister, a medical student at Oxford University, believed that he could run a mile in under four minutes. He was dismissed by other athletes and the scientific community as detached, unrealistic. On May 6, 1954, Roger Bannister broke the world record for the mile, running the distance in three minutes and fifty-nine seconds. The impossible had become reality.

But there is more: Only six weeks after Bannister's achievement, John Landy, an Australian runner, ran the mile in three minutes and fifty-eight seconds. A year later, three runners broke the four-minute barrier *in a single race.* Since 1954, the four-minute mile has been surpassed thousands of times. The impenetrable barrier, it turned out, was a product of the mind—and it was broken by the mind.

The lesson to be learned from the story of Roger Bannister is that our beliefs—whether we are optimistic or pessimistic—play a significant role in creating our reality. This does not mean that we can throw reality out the window and that everything that we hope and wish for will come true, but it does imply that we are more in control of our life than we sometimes dare to believe.

Where do your beliefs limit you? What barriers can you overcome on your way to fulfilling your dreams?

30.

ESTABLISH YOUR SUPERIORITY

—*or*—

Make others feel good

I've learned that people will forget what you said, people will forget what you did, but people will never forget how you made them feel.

—Maya Angelou

We tend to feel better about ourselves when we think that we are better than others; we feel good about ourselves when others recognize that we are good. Like peacocks, we have the tendency to flaunt our superior beauty or intelligence or ability. And while there is nothing wrong with wanting to be admired and respected—our nature is such that we care about others' opinions—this desire to flaunt can come at the expense of other people. When, to feel superior, we make others feel inferior, we hurt them (and, in the long run, ourselves). A healthy and stable self-esteem cannot come at the expense of others' self-esteem; a deep and lasting positive regard for ourselves can only emerge from making others feel better about themselves.[30]

JEFF BEZOS, FOUNDER AND CEO of Amazon, spent his summers working on his grandparents' ranch in Texas, fixing windmills, vaccinating cattle, and performing other chores. One summer, when he was ten years old, Jeff joined his grandparents on a road trip. His grandfather drove, while his grandmother sat in the passenger seat, smoking the whole time.

Jeff had always been fascinated by numbers. He had recently read that every puff on a cigarette takes two minutes from your life. Roughly estimating how many puffs per day his grandmother takes, and multiplying it by the number of days she had been smoking, Jeff tapped his grandmother on her shoulder and proudly declared, "At two minutes per puff, you've taken nine years off of your life." He expected to be applauded for his cleverness, for his arithmetic skills, but that is not what happened. Instead, his grandmother burst into tears.

His grandfather stopped the car, and he and Jeff got out. In a gentle, soft voice, he told the boy, "Jeff, one day you'll understand that it's harder to be kind than clever."

Thirty-five years later, in 2010, Jeff addressed the graduating class at Princeton University. After sharing with them this story, he said: "What I want to talk to you about today is the difference between gifts and choices. Cleverness is a gift; kindness is a choice. Gifts are easy; they are given, after all. Choices can be hard."

Before showing off your gifts to others, give them the gift of kindness.

31.

DWELL ON WEAKNESSES AND DEFICIENCIES

—or—

Focus on strengths and abilities

It's abilities, not the disabilities, that count.
—Peter Drucker

Individuals who invest in their strengths are happier and more successful. This does not mean that we should ignore our weaknesses but, rather, that our primary focus ought to be that which we are naturally good at. In the words of leadership expert Peter Drucker, "Only when you operate from strengths, can you achieve true excellence."

The kind of questions that I have to ask myself if I am to discover my strengths are: What are my strengths? What am I naturally good at? Where do my talents reside? What are my unique abilities? These questions are significant for choosing general life goals (being a writer, becoming a teacher, pursuing a career in law, and so on) as well as for choosing to apply my strengths in the immediate future (prepare a speech for my employees, hone my math skills, plan a family vacation, and so on).[31]

IN THEIR BOOK *Soar with Your Strengths,* Donald Clifton and Paula Nelson tell the parable of a new school in the forest, aimed at helping the young animals become well rounded.

On the first day, the little rabbit came to school and was put in running and hopping classes, which he was great at and loved; he came home after school excited and could hardly wait to return to school the following day. On the second day, the teachers put the rabbit in flying and swimming classes, which he struggled with and absolutely hated; he felt like a failure and came home disheartened and depressed. When he told his parents that he wanted to quit school, his parents told him that he must continue because his future success depended on becoming well rounded.

When he returned to school, he was given extra lessons in swimming and flying, because he needed to improve in those areas; his running and hopping classes were canceled because he was already good at these subjects and no extra work was necessary.

This parable unfortunately captures the reality, or part of the reality, in most organizations—from schools to businesses. Although it is certainly true that we should not ignore our weaknesses—we need to learn to write, do basic arithmetic, and acquire some skills at work just to get by in the world; at the same time we must not ignore our strengths—and invest most of our efforts cultivating our talents and abilities.

We need to invest in our weaknesses so that we can survive in the world; we need to invest in our strengths so that we can thrive.

Take some time to think about your strengths, those things that you are good at, those areas where your talents reside. Once you identify your strengths, find ways to use them more often in your daily life.

32.

TIGHTEN UP

—or—

Let go

> *Some of us think holding on makes us strong; but sometimes it is letting go.*
>
> —Hermann Hesse

My body and my mind constitute a single, unified system. Anything that affects one component of the system usually affects the other as well. Every emotional or psychological state has an impact on our physical being—for better and for worse. This means that if I'm experiencing tension in my throat, it is usually a sign of emotional stress; and letting go of the tension—releasing the physical pressure—may alleviate the emotional stress. Clenched jaws are often a sign of deep-seated anger (of which we may not even be aware). Simply relaxing the tension of the jaw can help release some of the anger.

To let go of the physical tension—be it in my forehead, jaw, throat, shoulders, belly, or back—I can shift my focus to that part of the body, breathe into it, and release it. I can even utter to myself in silence to let go as I relieve myself of the tension and strain, and gently sink into calmness and tranquility.[32]

PATRICIA WALDEN, THE RENOWNED yoga teacher, says that the most important part of a yoga practice is the end, when practitioners lie down flat on their back, hands to their side resting on the floor, legs straight and comfortably relaxed. This pose, called *sivasana* (corpse), is about yielding to the force of gravity and allowing the floor to support us. We let go of the tension and release the pressure in every part of our body. Through this we can also release the psychological tension we may be holding on to.

Sivasana rarely fails to induce a sense of calm and relaxation. However, its value goes beyond the immediate sensation, as the calm it brings us is transportable. Once we are familiar with the feeling of relaxation, we can replicate it in other areas of our life. And the more we enter this state in the controlled environment—on the yoga mat, a bed, or the floor—the more easily we can experience it in other situations. Those who have practiced this form of relaxation are able to experience the same sense of calm, in almost any place and at almost any time, simply by telling themselves to let go.

Wherever you are, whether in a work meeting, sitting with your partner, holding your child, or writing a report, you can relax any part of your body that feels tight, release any tension that you may be holding on to. And because mind and body are one, by becoming aware of your body and by learning to let go of the tension that it holds within it, your whole being becomes calmer and more serene.

33.

FOCUS ON OUTCOME

—or—

Focus on process

It is good to have an end to journey towards, but it is the journey that matters in the end.
—Ursula K. Le Guin

A considerable amount of research in psychology suggests that our mental health is to a great extent a function of our sense of control over our own life. At the same time, it is no less important to our mental health for us to accept that we have no control over certain things. These two seemingly conflicting needs—the need to control and the need to release control—have an important role to play in every project that we undertake in life, from preparing a report for our boss to planning a surprise party. Respecting the boundaries of these needs is essential to our health.

We have control over the goals we set and over the effort that we invest in them, but success is largely beyond our control. Therefore, it is important to stop trying to control the outcome, and to instead focus as much as possible on the process of arriving at that outcome.[33]

DURING THE THIRD YEAR of my PhD program—when the challenging qualifying exams were ahead and I was about to start the research stage—I went through a stressful period. I was not sure that I would pass the qualifying exams (having already failed similar exams once before), and I had not yet figured out what my dissertation would be about. The uncertainty of the entire situation stressed me out. I realized that I was stressed because I felt a need to control something that was beyond my power to control: the future.

What ultimately helped me get through this period of my life was learning to live with the lack of control. At the same time, I started to focus a lot more on those things that I did have control over. I could control whether I read or did coursework on a particular afternoon, or whether I sat down in front of the computer to write when I got up in the morning.

The lesson from that period is still with me every day, and every moment, whether I'm working on strategy for a company I'm consulting for, spending time with my family on our vacation, or writing a book on choice.

Can you let go of outcome and focus on the process? Can you, rather than obsessing over reaching the destination, pay attention to the journey?

34.

PERCEIVE HARDSHIP AS PERMANENT

—or—

Perceive hardship as temporary

> *Whatever comes, this too shall pass away.*
>
> —Ella Wheeler Wilcox

Our life is not free from sorrow and suffering. Even the happiest person in the world experiences sadness, disappointment, anger, and grief. The difference between happy and unhappy people is not whether they experience painful emotions—everyone does—but how they approach these emotions and how they interpret their experiences. People who are unhappy tend to believe that painful emotions are here to stay—which, of course, they are more likely to if this is their expectation. By contrast, happy people know that painful emotions—like all emotions—are temporary, and this expectation tends to liberate them from their unpleasant experience.

When we choose to perceive painful experiences as they truly are—as temporary and fleeting—then we allow them to take their natural course. Just as these emotions arrived naturally, so they will naturally depart.[34]

THERE IS A STORY, told in various traditions, about a king who could not banish his sorrow. No matter what he tried—the remedies prepared by his doctors, the advice offered by his wise counselors—he continued to be unhappy, becoming more despondent every day that passed.

In desperation, messengers were sent out across the land, promising a reward to anyone who could help the king. The greatest experts came to the palace and tried their best, but to no avail.

A few days later, an old man dressed in work clothes arrived at the palace gate. "I am a farmer," he said, "and a student of nature. I have come to help the king."

"The king doesn't need help from the likes of you!" the king's chief counselor said dismissively.

"I shall wait, then, until he is prepared to see me."

With each passing day, the king's condition worsened. He felt sad and helpless, and he saw no end to his suffering. Finally, when virtually all hope was lost, the counselor let the old man in. Without uttering a word, the man approached the king, handed him a simple wooden ring, and left. The king looked at the ring, read the inscription that was etched on it, and slipped it on his finger. For the first time in months he smiled.

"What does it say, Your Majesty?" asked the king's counselor.

"Just four words," said the king. "'This, too, shall pass.'"

When you experience unhappiness, remind yourself that this, too, shall pass.

35.

REMAIN INACTIVE

—or—

Move

> *Having a bout of exercise is like taking a little bit of Prozac and a little bit of Ritalin, right where it is supposed to go.*
>
> —John Ratey

Being active contributes to our physical health, significantly reducing the likelihood of heart disease, diabetes, and cancer. But the benefits from being active are not limited to the body. A moderate amount of physical exercise on a regular basis—as little as thirty minutes three times a week—has the same effect in combating depression and anxiety as does the most powerful psychiatric medication. Being active increases overall psychological well-being, enhances concentration and creativity, and significantly reduces the likelihood of dementia and cognitive impairment later in life. To increase the likelihood of enjoying physical and mental health, we need to move it.[35]

IN THE FILM *WALL-E,* society has reached a stage where people are so overweight and their muscles so atrophied that they are hardly able to walk. They spend their days lying down, fed by machines, mindlessly watching whatever is showing on the big screen in front of them. Sadly, over the past few decades we have taken immense strides toward this dystopian future.

Today, unlike in the not-too-distant past, we can afford the "luxury" of being lazy. We no longer need to run after a deer for lunch or run away from a lion so that we don't become lunch; we heat up our supper or have it warmed up for us and delivered to our doorstep. We no longer need to cut trees to warm up our cave, but simply press a switch to turn on the heat. We can—and many of us do—spend our days in front of the computer or on the phone, and our evenings glued to the TV. Children today, rather than playing on the street or in the fields as children did only a few decades ago, spend most of their waking hours physically idle in front of one screen or another.

Our nature requires us to be physically active, just as it requires us to breathe oxygen and eat the right food. When we frustrate a natural need, we pay a high price, physically and psychologically. The unnatural new world of *WALL-E* is closer than ever, and we must avert the onslaught of slothfulness by moving and encouraging others to do the same.

Enjoying the benefits of exercise does not require a radical change of lifestyle. Small changes to your routine can make a big difference. Choose to park a few hundred yards away from your office, take up gardening, use the stairs instead of the elevator a few times a week. These light activities will add up, and will contribute to your physical and mental health.

36.

ACT LIKE A KNOW-IT-ALL

—or—

Open your mind and heart to learning

> *The most common source of mistakes in management decisions is the emphasis on finding the right answer rather than the right question.*
>
> —PETER DRUCKER

TO KNOW IS TO arrive; to ask questions is to embark on a quest. People whose lives are characterized by a question mark rather than a period, who look for learning opportunities everywhere they go, are generally happier, are more creative, enjoy better relationships, and attain higher levels of success.

To be a lifelong learner is both fun and functional, and all we need to travel along that path is a humble heart and a curious mind. Every person we meet—a student or a teacher, a friend or a stranger—can teach us something; each experience holds within it an important lesson; in every moment is a message waiting to be discovered. When we embrace the spirit of inquiry and curiosity, we embrace life. How wonderful it is that this life is an inexhaustible source of wonders.

How exciting to learn that the excitement of learning can last a lifetime.[36]

THE ANALECTS IS A collection of short books capturing the words and deeds of Confucius, the great Chinese philosopher. They emphasize the importance of keeping an open mind and an open heart. In chapter 15 of the third book, Confucius enters the Grand Temple and proceeds to ask questions about everything. One of those present comments that this behavior is inappropriate form: A great scholar should not ask so many questions about trivial matters. Confucius overhears the comment and says, "This, too, is correct form." The Great Master understands the importance of opening one's mind and heart, and humbly exemplifies this behavior.

Kung Wen-tzu, a contemporary of Confucius, was crafty and sought power in his life, and yet was given the title Wen—meaning "cultured"—after he died. In book five, one of Confucius's disciples asks why such a person was given that honor posthumously. Confucius responds that it was due to his love of learning and his openness to learn from all people, regardless of their rank.

Less than one hundred years after Confucius, the great Greek philosopher Socrates displayed a similar openness to learning, when he acknowledged that his wisdom is predicated on the fact that he knows that he does not know.

Open your heart and mind to the wealth of knowledge that is all around you. Ask questions, listen, learn.

37.

LOSE SIGHT OF WHAT TRULY MATTERS

—or—

Connect to your values

> *The most precious things in life are not those you get for money.*
>
> —Albert Einstein

THE DEMANDS OF THE day-to-day, the hectic pace of modern life, the numbing monotone of routine—these often obscure from our eyes the things that are truly valuable to us. And so we make our way through life without the feeling of being alive. We feel lethargic, enervated, because we forget what a privilege it is to be alive, to be in possession of so many priceless gifts.

To wake up, to regain our zest for life, we can remind ourselves of the things that truly matter, of those things that make life worth living. Is it a particular child, or the laughter of children? A dear friend? Is it what we get to spend our time on at work or home? Is it our ability to smell a flower, taste the sweetness of a fruit, listen to a symphony, or feel love? Is it merely being alive? What do we have—right now, right here—that is more valuable to us than all the gold in the world?[37]

RABBI NOAH WEINBERG HAS helped thousands of people regain their love of life by reminding them to focus on the things that truly matter. Here's a variation on one of his stories.

Imagine that you are an investment banker. The past few months have been awful, with the market going through one of its worst periods ever. One day at work you make a bad decision that ends up costing you a lot of money. You get home, feeling exhausted and upset. Your partner, who also had a hard day at work and has just spent a few hours with the children, asks you to go through the bedtime routine with them.

You ask your six-year-old to take a bath and he refuses to do so; your four-year-old follows her big brother and is equally unruly. You're exasperated, ready to give up.

You hear a knock. You walk to the door, open it, and in front of you see an elderly gentleman, well dressed, holding a briefcase. "How can I help you?" you ask him, to which he responds, "I'm actually here to help you!"

He continues, "I know you are going through a rough period, and I'd like to offer you one hundred million dollars for your kids." As he speaks, he opens up the briefcase, which is packed with one-hundred-dollar bills. "Your kids will be well taken care of—I have a list of credible guarantors—and you will be able to visit them once a month." Needless to say, you throw the person out of your home—even though your financial concerns and your troubles with your kids could be over in a minute.

We needn't wait for a knock on the door to remind us what truly matters to us, of all the priceless things in our life.

38.

FLY THROUGH LIFE ON AUTOPILOT

—or—

Choose deliberately

> *I am the master of my fate: I am the captain of my soul.*
>
> —William Ernest Henley

We spend much of our time "flying on autopilot," reacting unthinkingly in the same way we always have in the past to whatever it is that life throws at us. We may get angry when someone says something we strongly disagree with; we may withdraw affection when we are criticized; we may give up when a challenge seems daunting. In the moment, these reactions may feel inevitable, but they are not.

When I go through life reacting to everything in the same way I always have before, I deny myself the possibility of much more positive experiences. Instead, I need to step back and think about how I want to respond to a situation. I need to take control and act consciously and deliberately, thus creating a better experience for myself and for those around me.[38]

THERE IS ALWAYS ONE relative who knows how to push your buttons. At family get-togethers, this person somehow always manages to say the things that are guaranteed to upset or irritate you, and you let your irritation show. Perhaps you even enter into arguments with your relative, both sides saying things that don't get you anywhere. This might happen again and again, each time leaving a bad taste in your mouth for the rest of the day.

What if, at the next family reunion, you refuse to rise to the bait? Stop and remind yourself that you are not a prisoner of the situation (or of your relative), that there are a number of other ways to react that you haven't tried yet. You can choose to completely ignore this person, or to joke with him that you're getting too old to keep going at it. Or tell this relative that you'd like to think about his point of view some more, and that right now you'd like to enjoy the precious time you have together.

Modify your usual reaction even slightly, and you might find that you are piloting yourself and those around you on a different course—a much more pleasant journey.

39.

FROWN

—or—

Smile

> *Sometimes your joy is the source of your smile, but sometimes your smile can be the source of your joy.*
>
> —Thích Nhất Hạnh

MIND AND BODY ARE interconnected. What we do with our body impacts our thoughts and feelings, and in turn, these influence our physiological reactions. Research into what psychologists call the "facial feedback hypothesis" shows that we can affect our own mood through our facial expressions—a smile will bring about a more positive feeling, whereas a frown will make us feel worse. In fact, we can improve our mood at almost any point by simply smiling, or better, laughing. To jump-start the process we may think of something that makes us smile—someone we love, a funny story or situation—or just mechanically *fake* the smile until we *make* the emotion real.[39]

MY WORK INVOLVES TWO major activities—writing and public speaking. Last year I spoke to over fifty different audiences, ranging in size from a handful of people to several thousand. I love being able to interact directly with students, clients, and other groups of people who are interested in the science of well-being. But public speaking did not come naturally or easily to me. I am essentially a shy and introverted person. When I first started teaching, just *thinking* about standing in front of a classroom would cause my heart to pound and my throat to go dry. These physical symptoms would become particularly acute, practically paralyzing, just before the lecture began. But I refused to allow my physical reactions to prevent me from pursuing my calling, even though I was aware that they had a negative impact on the quality of my teaching.

One of the techniques that I have found most useful in overcoming my stage fright—an issue I still wrestle with even though I've been delivering lectures for more than two decades—is to make a choice to genuinely smile before I go onstage. I think of something funny or pleasant, or I think of a person I love, or I remind myself how fortunate I am to be sharing the subject that I care about most with others. My body fills up with those naturally created feel-good love chemicals (oxytocin and others), and I actually feel happier and more upbeat. I am able to express the genuine excitement and passion I feel for the subject of my lecture, instead of using all my energy just to push myself through the first few slides. If, for one reason or another, I become nervous in the middle of a presentation, I again generate a genuine smile and by doing so invariably bring myself back to center.

My smile-inspired positive mood also helps the audience to relax and relate positively to me and my subject, leading to a better experience for everyone. By making a deliberate choice to smile instead of focusing on my anxiety, I improve everyone's experience—and that increases the likelihood that when the presentation is over, I will still be smiling.

40. SEE THE GLASS AS HALF EMPTY

—or—

See the glass as half full

> *Every person, place, and thing has something of value, some worth, some untapped opportunity; one simply has to inquire into it.*
>
> —Jacqueline Stavros and Cheri Torres

When we focus on the deficiencies of an organization, or the defects of a person, or the downside of a situation, we are magnifying those aspects that do not work, at the expense of those that do. But when we actively seek out those things that work, we amplify the positive. A healthy life requires a realistic perspective—one that does not ignore problems, and at the same time, does not ignore when things are going well.

Our culture tends to highlight the negative and underplay the positive, leading to a distorted view of reality. The underlying cause of this biased perspective is to some extent the news media, which by and large plays the role of a magnifying glass (selectively focusing on the negative) rather than a looking glass (accurately representing reality). While there is certainly a value to the media's negative focus—playing the role of a watchdog—there are unhealthy side effects in the form of a distorted worldview. To counter this bias toward the empty part of the glass, we need to be hypervigilant about identifying the part of the glass that is full.[40]

IN THE CLASSIC MOVIE *It's a Wonderful Life,* George, the protagonist, is about to commit suicide, feeling that his life is meaningless and worthless; but then his guardian angel, Clarence, gets ahold of him and decides to teach him a lesson.

Clarence reminds George of the good deeds that he had committed, such as saving his brother's life when he almost drowned, and convincing a bank to continue providing home loans to poor people. Clarence shows George what the world would have been like had he not been born. George realizes that his small contributions went a long way to making the world a better place. George is then able to return to his real life more appreciative of what he has, and more likely to focus on the wonderful, positive aspects of his existence.

Although we may not all have saved someone's life or fought the banks on behalf of poor homeowners, we can all find aspects of our life that are positive, wonderful. We are so often focused on the empty part of the glass that we miss the great and small treasures in our daily life. It often takes a wake-up call, a shift in perspective—inspired by our guardian angel or by ourselves—to remind us that even with all the difficulties and disappointments, there is still much to celebrate.

What can you celebrate right now? What do you see when you focus on the positive aspects of your life, the treasures, the full part of the glass?

41.

LIVE IN THE PAST OR THE FUTURE

—or—

Be present

Forever is composed of nows.
—Emily Dickinson

We spend so much of our short lives haunted by the *what if,* rather than luxuriating in the *what is*—in the tense "hypothetical future" rather than in the calm, real present. What if I don't do well on the exam? What if I don't get a promotion? Rather than fully experiencing the here and now, we are, in the words of poet Galway Kinnell, "smearing the darkness of expectation across experience." Alternatively, we spend so much of our time stuck in the past, rehearsing unsatisfying histories, brooding over a failed relationship or project that did not work out as planned. Rather than allowing ourselves to remain enslaved by our past or future, we can choose a life in which we luxuriate in the fullness of feeling that the present brings.[41]

IN THEIR BOOK *Appreciative Coaching,* Sara Orem, Jacqueline Binkert, and Ann Clancy tell the story of Rory, a medical secretary who decided to leave the security of his job to pursue his passion by creating a yoga studio and massage business. Shortly after embarking on his new path, Rory began to experience anxiety, thinking constantly about his past failures and the uncertain future. He was, as writer Fulton Oursler puts it, torn between "regret for yesterday and fear of tomorrow." What if there was no interest? What if he had no clients?

Realizing that his negative *what if* thinking was dragging him down, Rory did a very simple thing: he painted the word *now* in bold lettering on the face of his watch. Each time he looked at his watch, it reminded him that the time is now, that life is in the present rather than the past or the future. This simple act—similar to having a wristband reminding us of something important—changed the way he experienced and lived his life. Rory became more positive, energized, and ultimately more successful. By focusing on the present, "Rory came to realize that each present moment was pregnant with possibility and choice for him."

Remind yourself to focus on the here and now—start wearing a wristband, paint the word *now* on your watch, or have a screensaver on your computer or phone that you associate with being present. Even a minute of centering every few hours—a minute during which you focus on your breathing or on some other physical sensation (or even your physical surroundings)—can go a long way toward improving the quality of your entire day.

42.

DELAY GRATIFICATION

—or—

Seize the moment

> *Pleasure for man is not a luxury, but a profound psychological need.*
>
> —Nathaniel Branden

Learning to delay gratification is important. It is a critical step in our development as children, and there is considerable research that shows that it is a prerequisite for success in life and for overall psychological health. However, in our fast-paced, crazy-busy world, we sometimes delay gratification so much that our life becomes barren: dull, unexciting, devoid of passion. If we delay gratification indefinitely, we end up with no gratification at all, because we do not live indefinitely. Taking three minutes to listen to our favorite song even though our inbox is overflowing, spending an hour with our best friend despite the looming deadline at work, or going to the movies when our world seems to be falling apart—these may be irresponsible things to do, or they may be the best things that we can do for ourselves and others. These brief activities are what we often need to refuel, to replenish our energy stores.[42]

THE MOST SIGNIFICANT INCREASE that I experienced in my level of well-being was not a result of a large-scale transformational change in my life; rather, it was due to my introducing what I've come to call happiness boosters—bite-size activities that elevate my mood. These mini-breaks provide me the fuel that I need to continue to function with energy and zest.

Today, I often close my eyes for a minute and imagine a person I love, or if I have more time, I sit down and go through a twenty-minute loving kindness meditation. I will take a few minutes out of my schedule to listen to Whitney Houston's "I Will Always Love You," or I will allow myself a longer break to savor all five movements in Beethoven's Sixth Symphony. I may take three deep breaths or decide to take a short nap. I may read a brief poem by Pablo Neruda or take an hour to enjoy Robert Heinlein's fantastic imagination.

In the past, I often reached a point where I felt depleted, when I had little enthusiasm for work (and sometimes even for life in general). The best cure, I found, was to inject a few happiness boosters into my daily routine. Today, rather than waiting for my energy levels to drop dangerously low before I take a break, I incorporate instant gratification into my life on a regular basis. These infusions of moments of joy do not merely make me feel better in the moment, they often create a current of enthusiasm and energy that helps me become more productive, more creative, happier.

The challenge, as it often is, is to find the right balance between delaying gratification, and grabbing it. I leave that to you . . .

43.

DO WHAT YOU FEEL THAT YOU HAVE TO DO

—or—

Do what you want to do

> *How we spend our days is, of course,*
> *how we spend our lives.*
> —ANNIE DILLARD

GOALS THAT ARE ALIGNED with my ideals and interests—ones that I choose freely—lead to greater success and well-being than do goals that I pursue because I feel that I have to. This does not mean that I should shirk my responsibilities or avoid meeting my obligations because I don't feel like carrying them through at a particular moment. Rather, it means that I should construct my life as a whole so that the path my life takes is the one that I actively choose for myself. It means that to the extent possible—taking into consideration all the limitations and constraints that we all face in life—I pursue my passions and am true to my values and desires.[43]

PSYCHOLOGISTS ELLEN LANGER AND Judith Rodin conducted research in an old-age home where they randomly assigned residents of two floors to two different groups. Those who lived on one particular floor received all the support they needed—everything was done for them, from organizing their schedules to watering their plants. The group on the other floor was given some responsibility and choice. For example, they chose a plant and cared for it themselves; they had more choice over decisions in their own lives such as when they would watch movies, where to receive their guests, and so on. They had more opportunities to choose what it was that they *wanted* to do.

Eighteen months later, those who were part of the group that had more choice over their daily routine were, both in their own eyes and in the eyes of their caregivers, significantly healthier, more active, less depressed, and more confident, alert, and cheerful.

Perhaps the most striking result of the study was that the survival rate of members of the group given responsibility and choice was double that of the control group. In other words, watering plants, choosing which movie to watch, and other seemingly trivial choices not only improved their quality of life, but significantly increased their life span as well!

Rather than trying to help people—young or old—by catering to their every need, we need to provide them with choices. A life can be transformed when we move from *have to* to *want to,* from prescribed activities to freely chosen ones—not just of the elderly, but of twenty- or ten-year-olds, too. Small decisions make a big difference.

Life is short. What do you want to do with your life right now? Tomorrow? Ten years from now?

44.

AVOID MAKING MISTAKES BY NOT TRYING

—*or*—

Learn from failure

If you want to increase your success rate, double your failure rate.
—THOMAS WATSON

WHEN WE HEAR ABOUT extremely successful people, we mostly hear about their great accomplishments—not about the many mistakes they made and the failures they experienced along the way. In fact, the most successful people throughout history are also those who have had the most failures. That is no coincidence. People who achieve great feats, no matter in what field, understand that failure is not a stumbling block but a stepping-stone on the road to success. There is no success without risk and failure. We often fail to see this truth because the outcome is more visible than the process—we see the final success and not the many failures that led to it.

When I acknowledge that fulfilling my potential must involve some failure, I no longer run away from risks and challenges. The choice is a simple one: Learn to fail, or fail to learn.[44]

THOMAS EDISON HAD 1,093 patents registered to his name—more than any other person in history! And while he most certainly deserves a place of honor in the science hall of fame, he also deserves honorary membership in the "failure hall of fame" for the tens of thousands of experiments he conducted that failed. Edison himself, however, did not see these experiments as failures. When he was working on one of his inventions, a storage battery, someone pointed out to him that he had failed ten thousand times. "I have not failed," responded Edison, "I've just found ten thousand ways that won't work." Recognizing the real path to his accomplishments, Edison remarked, "I failed my way to success."

Another honorary member, alongside Edison, is Babe Ruth, whom most North Americans know for topping the league in home runs. But how many also know that he topped the league five times in strikeouts? To take an example from a different field of activity, Abraham Lincoln failed in business several times, had a nervous breakdown at age twenty-seven, and lost eight elections for political office, all before becoming one of the most celebrated presidents in the history of the United States.

Are there areas in your life where the fear of failure is holding you back? Where can you exit your comfort zone and take a step toward realizing your potential?

45.

REMAIN INDIFFERENT

—or—

Help and contribute

You can always, always give something,
even if it is only kindness.
—Anne Frank

WITH EVER-INCREASING DEMANDS ON our time, energy, and resources, many of us feel that we are doing all we can just to meet our obligations. As a result, we often let pass the opportunities that we have to help other people. Crucially, it's not only those in need who pay the price of our indifference. We, too, lose out by not helping others.

Psychologist Sonja Lyubomirsky conducted an experiment in which she asked people to carry out, in the course of one day, five kind acts that they would not normally do. These actions do not have to be grand and dramatic (though if you can do something to bring about world peace, that would be great). An act of kindness can be baking cookies for your neighbor, or donating money or time to a cause you believe in, or helping a friend think through a dilemma, or giving blood, or even simply opening a door for a stranger. What Lyubomirsky found was that whether large or small, these acts of kindness contributed significantly to the well-being of those who gave, not just while they were performing these acts, not just for that one day, but for the entire week.[45]

THREE TEENAGERS—DORON HARMAN, Israela Bar Shishat, and Hodaya Aflalo—participated in an Israeli program called LEAD, a program that teaches high school students leadership skills and encourages them to contribute to their community. As their final project, the three chose to help mentally challenged individuals, a population that actually receives quite a lot of assistance from a range of special programs, as well as from social workers, volunteers, and their families. What the teenagers felt this population was missing was the opportunity to give rather than receive, and they set out to find ways to enable the group of mentally challenged individuals to contribute to the community.

The impact of this intervention—helping those who usually rely on others' contributions themselves become contributors—was remarkable in terms of the participants' sense of self-worth, well-being, and ultimately, their ability to help themselves. The project and the outcome illustrate the need—a need we *all* have—to help and contribute.

Often, the best way to help ourselves is to help others. By being generous in giving and generous in receiving we create win-win relationships, where helping and being helped interlace to form a web of empathy.

Where can you help? What can you do to contribute to others?

46.

TAKE SHORT, SHALLOW BREATHS

—or—

Breathe deeply and slowly

> *If I had to limit my advice on healthier living to just one tip, it would be simply to learn how to breathe correctly.*
>
> —Andrew Weil

Shallow breathing is a reaction to the unyielding stress of modern life—and is itself a cause of further stress, which leads to more shallow breathing. To stop this downward spiral of shallow breathing and stress—even in the midst of the daily mayhem—I can take three or four deep breaths and enter an upward spiral of deep breathing and calm. I can switch on the healing power of deep breathing right now and at any time throughout my day—as I wake up, while on the train, in the middle of a meeting, before going to sleep, while waiting for the red light to turn green, or while reading a book. All I need to do is gently, without strain, fill up the space of my belly, and then slowly and tenderly breathe out.[46]

THOMAS CRUM, IN HIS book *Three Deep Breaths,* follows Angus, a busy man who is unsuccessfully trying to achieve work-life balance. Angus is torn between his desire to spend quality time with his wife and daughter, and the relentless demands of his work. And he ends up feeling frustrated in both spheres. He experiences constant stress, guilt, anger, and fatigue.

One morning, when everything seems to be going wrong, Angus meets an old man who becomes his teacher. The old man helps Angus regain his center, by introducing him to the three-deep-breaths technique. This scientifically based technique is simple, and it can help us all shift from the fight-or-flight response to what Herbert Benson calls the "relaxation response."

I use a variation of Thomas Crum's technique, and it has done wonders for me. I take a first belly breath—breathing slowly and deeply, expanding my stomach as I breathe in—and I focus on centering, on being present in the here and now. I take a second deep belly breath, and while doing so focus on my purpose—whether for that day or for my life as a whole. The third deep breath is dedicated to something for which I'm grateful—thinking about a family member, a meeting I had or am about to have, or anything else.

The physiological impact of deep breathing, coupled with the cognitive component of focusing on something positive, provides a powerful technique that can change the way you feel. The technique is particularly effective in bringing about calm and joy if you do it a few times a day.

47.

LASH OUT AT THOSE CLOSE TO YOU

—or—

Respect those close to you

Respect is love in plain clothes.

—FRANKIE BYRNE

OFTEN WE SAVE OUR best behavior for strangers. We tend to take greater liberties with those who are closest to us—those who care about us most and about whom we care—than we do with total strangers. We may say painful and hurtful things to family members; we may act hostile to our partner or best friend. Although such lashing out may come from a feeling of intimacy and a long shared history (and no worthwhile relationship is going to be free of friction, and at times, pain), there is no justification for insults, hostility, or contempt. I therefore propose a slightly modified version of the Golden Rule: Do not do unto those close to you what you would not have done unto others (who are not so close to you). We can get angry and upset, we can be disappointed and hurt, but if we want our relationships to flourish over time, we must treat those we love with at least as much respect as we do those we have just met.[47]

I COME FROM AN Orthodox Jewish family, and when I reached the grand old age of eighteen, my grandmother started putting pressure on me to get married. After about a year of introducing me to "nice Jewish girls"—mostly granddaughters of her friends—without apparent results, she sat me down for a serious talk.

My problem, she explained to me, was that I was looking for too much in one person. She told me a story about a young man from Sighet, the town in Romania she came from, who went to see a matchmaker when he was eighteen. The matchmaker asked the young man, "What is it that you are looking for in a wife?" The young man said that he wanted a woman from a good family, intelligent, good-hearted, attractive, humble, and a good cook. The matchmaker exclaimed, "You are out of your mind! With that long list of qualities, I could find husbands for six women." My grandmother told me this story to convey a simple point: No one's perfect; no one has it all.

When we are children, we often think that our parents are perfect. The same thing happens when we fall in love. But at some point, reality sets in, and we discover that the object of our affection is human, just like us! And then—whether it's because of the disappointment, or because we know their shortcomings so intimately—we attack them more than we do other people.

Instead of focusing on our loved ones' imperfections and weaknesses, we need to highlight to ourselves those traits that we admire and appreciate, and treat them with the love and respect that they deserve from us.

My grandparents were happily married for fifty-three years. I think I know why.

48.

SWAY WITH THE WINDS OF APPROVAL

—or—

Maintain the strength of independence

> *The reward for conformity is that everyone likes you but yourself.*
>
> —Rita Mae Brown

I am a social animal, and as such, naturally care about what people think of me. But the fact that I care about others' opinions does not mean that I have to forgo my personal beliefs and conform. What do I do when my own and others' views differ, when the choice is between social approval and maintaining my independence? The healthy approach is, first, to accept that it matters to me what other people think, then to try and understand and evaluate these views that conflict with my own, and finally do what I believe is right—whether it leads to praise or criticism from the people I respect.

When I follow my internal compass, my North Star, I declare my independence and gain the approval that matters most—my own.[48]

A VARIATION ON ONE of Aesop's fables tells of a wise man whose son was ashamed to leave the house, because he thought other people would think him ugly. The father told him that he shouldn't worry so much what other people thought, and to follow his own mind and heart. To make the point, the father asked his son to join him on his trips to the market over the next few days.

On the first day, the father rode the donkey, and the child walked alongside. As they traveled they could hear passersby criticizing the father for making a small child walk in the heat of the day.

On the second day, the child rode the donkey, while the father walked alongside him. This time people commented about how disrespectful the child was for making an old man walk while he rode in comfort.

On the third day they entered the market, both walking alongside the donkey. They heard the people saying how stupid they were: "Do they not know that donkeys are for riding?"

The following day, both father and son rode on the donkey, and people expressed their indignation about how cruel they were to burden the animal in such a way.

On the fifth day they carried the donkey on their backs. Everyone in the market laughed and ridiculed them.

The wise man then turned to his son and said, "You see, regardless of what you do, there'll always be people who will disapprove. Therefore, don't worry about others' opinions, and do what you think is just and right."

49.

BE DRIVEN BY GUILT AND DUTY

—or—

Pursue your passion

> *Passion will move men beyond themselves, beyond their shortcomings, beyond their failures.*
>
> —Joseph Campbell

When I adhere to my inner voice, I am more likely to thrive than when I do things out of guilt or a sense of duty. The former energize me; the latter enervate me. I need to ask myself: What gives me strength? What energizes me? What are my passions? What does my inner voice say to me? These questions are important for choosing general life goals (pursuing the career that is right for me, finding the right work-life balance, and so on) as well as for choosing what I want to do in the next moment (spend time with my children, read for an hour, go to the gym, and so on).

When I pursue my passions, not only do I come alive, I am more likely to infuse those around me with positive energy.[49]

STEVE JOBS, COFOUNDER OF Apple, sold something more than computers and gadgets. He sold emotion and passion. When he first presented the iPad to the world, he repeatedly said, "It's just so amazing to hold." There was obviously a genuine love for the product, a real passion for what his company had created.

Years earlier, Jobs was fired from the company he started, and he considered leaving Silicon Valley altogether. However, he realized that, though he had been rejected, he still loved what he did, and he started over—this time with NeXT and Pixar, with the latter becoming a tremendous success.

Even if we have no aspiration to become the next high-tech megastar, we can all learn from the way Steve Jobs lived his life. In 2005, when he delivered the commencement speech at Stanford University, he shared some invaluable advice with the young graduates: "Your time is limited, so don't spend it living someone else's life . . . have the courage to follow your heart and intuition."

Pursuing your passions may or may not lead to material or public success; however, regardless of external success, life is short, and finding small ways to express your inner, authentic voice at work, at home, or with your friends is perhaps the most important thing you can do for yourself and the world.

50.

TAKE THE GOOD FOR GRANTED

—or—

Appreciate the good

Gratefulness is the measure of our aliveness.
Are we not dead to whatever we take for granted?
Surely to be numb is to be dead.

—David Steindl-Rast

The word *appreciate* has two meanings. The first is to be thankful—the opposite of taking something for granted—and the second is to increase in value, the way we say that assets appreciate when their value rises. When it comes to the role that appreciation plays in our life, both these meanings are relevant. Psychological research has repeatedly shown that when we are thankful for the good in our life, the good grows and we have more of it. The opposite, sadly, is also true: When we fail to appreciate the good, when we take it for granted, the good depreciates.

You might want to keep a gratitude journal, writing down five things for which you are grateful before you go to bed each night. Or you might simply make an effort to notice three good things as you go about your daily routine. By becoming aware of all that you are blessed with, by appreciating the good, more good things are likely to come your way.[50]

PSYCHOLOGISTS ROBERT EMMONS AND Michael McCullough conducted a series of studies in which they asked participants to write down on a daily basis at least five things for which they were grateful. The items listed each day didn't have to be important and profound (although they could be); they could be trivial pleasures or fleeting experiences. Participants' responses included everything from their parents to the Rolling Stones, from waking up in the morning to God.

Taking a minute each day to express gratitude turns out to have far-reaching consequences. Compared to the control group, the "grateful group" not only became more appreciative but also enjoyed higher levels of well-being and positive emotions: These individuals felt happier, more determined, more energetic, and more optimistic. They were also more generous and more likely to offer support to others. Finally, those who expressed gratitude also slept better, exercised more, and experienced fewer symptoms of physical illness.

How can it be that simply taking some time to appreciate the good in our life has such major positive effects? Emmons and McCullough suggest that being grateful triggers a positive spiral of growth and well-being. When you think of all you can be grateful for, when you take stock, you feel better. When you feel better, you become more open to—and are more likely to notice and pursue—positive experiences. You then have more to be grateful for, which in turn improves the quality of your life, and so on. You can begin this positive spiral of happiness at any moment by choosing to reflect on the things for which you are grateful.

When you appreciate the good, the good appreciates.

51.

SEEK CONSTANT STIMULATION

—or—

Embrace silence

> *I have discovered that all the unhappiness of men arises from one single fact, that they cannot stay quietly in their own room.*
>
> —Blaise Pascal

A plant needs space to flourish; devoid of space, its growth will be stilted or distorted. Human beings are no different: To learn, to grow—to flourish—we need space. One of the ways in which we can create space for ourselves is through silence. When we fill every moment of our life with sounds, we fail to realize our true potential. A moment of silent meditation, of solitude, of being alone without the distraction of outside stimulus, can help us see clearly and understand deeply. We need time away from the clatter of cars, stereos, hammers, and footsteps. And we sometimes need to get away from words—our own and others'.[51]

IN HIS BOOK *LILA*, Robert M. Pirsig discusses two distinct cultural approaches to silence. The protagonist is on a search for a better way of life, and he spends time with a Native American tribe. Native Americans, he notes, unlike those of us who have been brought up in Western civilization, "don't talk to fill time. When they don't have anything to say, they don't say it." They would sit for hours around the fire, and exchange few if any words; they would sometimes look at one another, and mostly look within. This is in stark contrast to the white European who feels a great deal of discomfort in the absence of words. Hence small talk was invented.

But it's not only the absence of words that lead to the silence that the Native American embraces; it is also the absence of man-made noise. Our world has become addicted to noise: Children need music to concentrate on their homework, families need the television in the background when they sit around the dinner table, people who work out need a constant rhythm to help them keep moving. Noise has become such a part of our life that we crave it when it is absent. Silence during a business meeting is considered unproductive, a waste of time. Silence in a classroom discussion is viewed as a sign of disengaged students and an uninspiring teacher. Silence during a get-together proclaims the party a flop.

A growing body of research points to the high price we pay for this constant aural stimulation. Silence is necessary to increase creativity, deeper connection to our environment and ourselves, healthier physical and mental development, and higher levels of happiness.

Empty your life of some of the noise; fill it up with more silence.

52.

SURRENDER YOUR BELIEFS AND VALUES

—or—

Be true to your self

> *This above all—to thine own self be true;*
> *and it must follow, as the night the day,*
> *thou canst not then be false to any man.*
> —WILLIAM SHAKESPEARE

TO BE TRUE TO myself requires knowing myself and being myself—knowing what is important to me, knowing my values, and then living in accordance with this knowing. According to Warren Bennis, "Until you truly know yourself, strengths and weaknesses, know what you want to do and why you want to do it, you cannot succeed in any but the most superficial sense of the word." And once I know who I am and what I am about, then comes the equally difficult task of being true to that self. At times, this means going against the grain, asserting myself, doing things that may not be popular and may beget censure and disapproval from others. However, there is no way to lead a full and fulfilling life without being genuine and real.[52]

THERE IS AN IDIOM in the Mishna, the Jewish text, which literally translates to: "The face of the generation is like the face of a dog." Figuratively, the idiom describes a rotten generation, a dark age, a period in which people have gone astray and pursued immoral paths.

The dog is used as a metaphor because of its behavior around its master. We often see that a dog, as soon as it is unleashed, runs ahead of its owner. Ostensibly, the dog is leading. In actuality, the dog is following, constantly looking for hints from its master as to the direction the master will take. Once the dog figures out the direction of the master, it races full steam ahead until it reaches the next fork in the road.

The dog conforms to the status quo rather than asserting its independence. As far as we know, dogs do not have the capacity to decide whether to conform or not; this is the way most dogs instinctively behave. Human beings are *potentially* different; we can choose whether to follow or lead, to conform to others' will or to assert our own.

A generation that behaves like a pack of dogs—blindly following and conforming—is in bad shape. Some of the most heinous crimes in history were committed as a result of conformity to an authoritarian figure or an ideology that was not questioned. This does not mean that we ought to oppose the status quo or conventions just for the sake of doing so; however, it does mean that we ought to know what we are about, and then act accordingly—whether or not it aligns with the norm.

In writing or with a person you trust, reflect on your values and the things you care about most—and then commit to living the kind of life that would embody these.

53.

IGNORE OTHERS

—*or*—

See the other

The opposite of love is not hate, it's indifference.
—Elie Wiesel

As we go through life, we encounter dozens of people every day. Each person we meet is a world unto him- or herself. But we pass all these people by, and our attitude to them is mostly instrumental: We notice only those aspects that may be of use to us. What would happen if we tried to see each person as a complete human being, rather than as a means to an end? What if we truly tried to get to know people, go beyond the masks and titles and labels, and see them for who they really are? We would notice the beauty within them, appreciate their value—and as a result, the world would seem to us (and it would actually be) better for it.

Over time, an unintended consequence of learning to truly see others would be that we would begin to see ourselves in a different light as well—as worthy human beings, independent of our instrumental value to others.[53]

FOR YEARS, I HAVE been lecturing about Marva Collins, the legendary Chicago schoolteacher. I describe the miracles that she performed with at-risk children, helping them realize the great potential that existed within them, potential that so often remains unrecognized, unappreciated, and tragically, ultimately unrealized. Although I admired her from afar for many years, I never initiated a meeting with her, possibly out of shyness. But when I reached forty, my friend C.J. Lonoff thought it was time for me to meet my heroine and role model, even if this meant venturing out of my comfort zone. So as a surprise birthday gift, C.J. organized a lunch with her.

I was in seventh heaven! C.J. and I sat in a restaurant for three hours with Marva Collins and her husband, George, and during that time I felt I was privileged to be in the presence of greatness. Marva Collins has the gift of breathing life and energy into every person she comes in contact with. When we sat down at the table, our waiter appeared lethargic and emotionally not present. All it took was a few words from Mrs. Collins—a few smiles, a question or two about his background and his goals in life—and his energy and self-confidence visibly increased. And when his shift was over and a new waitress took over, she, too, received the same treatment. Mrs. Collins's interest in people is genuine, and when she interacts with others, she wants to get to know and to enjoy the company of each person.

She is that way with everyone she meets for the first time, as well as with her husband of many years, her friends and acquaintances, and of course her students. She sees them, accepts them without preconceptions, and brings out the best in them. If one of the children she is teaching gets upset with her, for being too demanding or not letting them slack off, and vents their frustration by saying something like, "I hate you, Mrs. Collins," her response is, "That's okay, sweetheart, I love you enough for the both of us."

Look, really look, at the people around you. Can you see your friends for who they are? Are you able to truly see the value and worth of the people you meet every day?

54.

INSIST ON PERFECTION

—or—

Recognize when good enough will do

> *Settle for a choice that meets your core requirements rather than searching for the elusive best.*
>
> —Barry Schwartz

Most of us today have far more choices than our grandparents had. We can choose where to live, what to study, where to work, and whom to date. And when we go on a date, we have multiple outfits to choose from, a huge music collection, a long list of enticing restaurants, and then there is the menu the length of a book. While choice is undeniably good, there can be too much of a good thing: more is not always better. In a world of plenty and opportunity there is more cause for endless deliberation, regret, and dissatisfaction.

What do we do? We settle for good enough, and then learn to appreciate our imperfect choice. While settling for good enough when making a particular decision *may* compromise on the potential satisfaction we derive from the particular choice, not settling for good enough and always searching for the perfect choice will *definitely* lead to unhappiness and dissatisfaction.[54]

IN HIS BOOK *The Paradox of Choice,* Barry Schwartz distinguishes between *maximizers* and *satisficers.* Maximizers will settle for nothing less than perfection: the perfect meal at a restaurant, the perfect outfit, the perfect holiday, the perfect partner. They spend hours looking for the item of clothing that is just right, comparing price, quality, and fit among the endless range of options available. They agonize over where to go on vacation, searching and researching, reviewing again and again the decisions they come close to making but cannot quite bring themselves to finalize. The problem they face is that there is no perfect meal, no perfect vacation, no perfect person. And therefore, no matter how many choices they have and how much time they spend reviewing them, nothing can ever match up to the ideal. The maximizer's perfectionism inevitably leads to endless "if only"s and "what if"s—to disappointment, frustration, regret, and ultimately unhappiness.

By contrast, satisficers are content with what is "good enough." They accept the reality of life that perfection may not be attainable—it may not even exist—and even if it were, the cost of endlessly agonizing over each choice far outweighs the gains of being a maximizer. And although satisficers will sometimes regret a choice they made—we all make mistakes, and regret is a natural response—their overall approach is acceptance and appreciation of what they have rather than what they don't have.

Choose to be a satisficer rather than a maximizer! Paradoxically, you would be maximizing the likelihood of finding happiness.

55.

ACT ON YOUR EMOTION

—or—

Actively accept your emotion

> *The curious paradox is that when I accept myself just as I am, then I can change.*
>
> —Carl Rogers

When we experience a strong emotion, it often seems that the choice we have is between mindlessly reacting to the emotion or rejecting it. In fact, however, whenever we feel an emotion, no matter how powerful it is, we face two choices. Our first choice is whether to reject or accept the emotion, whether to suppress or acknowledge that which is. Accepting our emotion is not necessarily about liking everything that we feel; rather, it is about allowing ourselves to fully experience it. Our second choice is whether to automatically react to the emotion or to take the time to think about the most appropriate way to act in the given situation.

Active acceptance is about putting these two choices together: First, embracing the emotion rather than rejecting it; and second, rather than mindlessly reacting to that emotion, choosing the most appropriate course of action.[55]

LENNY RAVICH is an author and comedian. Recently, he told a story on stage about inviting his son, Nati, over for dinner to celebrate Nati's birthday. Nati's work and his young family made considerable demands on his time, so there hadn't been many opportunities for Lenny and Nati to spend quality time together lately. They were both looking forward to this special occasion.

Soon after they sat down, Nati's phone rang. He picked it up, and began a long conversation. As he sat and waited, Lenny felt resentment and anger building up inside him. Someone was taking away from him precious time with his son, on his birthday!

To deal with his emotions, Lenny decided to practice mindfulness—to become aware of what he was experiencing. As he observed the emotions within him, he realized that this mindfulness gave him a great gift: "It gave me the gift of choice." He could *choose* how to respond to this situation: "Should I hold my anger in, not say a word, wait until the next time the phone rings and interrupts us? Or should I tell him of my disappointment, probably hurting his feelings?"

When Nati's conversation ended, Lenny picked up his own phone and called his son. Nati looked at his phone, and saw who was calling him. "What are you calling me for? I'm sitting right here in front of you?" he said, half into the phone and half into the air between them. Lenny, with a big smile, responded: "Because I want to talk to you." Nati laughed. For the rest of that meal, and from then on, they'd smile at each other anytime the phone rang.

Lenny's situation could have exploded with his shame, blame, and anger, ruining the special occasion for father and son. But as Lenny was able to prove to himself, you always have the choice to observe an emotion before responding. And when you recognize and acknowledge it, you are in a better state of mind and heart to choose the most fitting response. Active acceptance can help us make better choices transform potentially negative experiences into positive ones.

56.

EXPERIENCE THE DULLNESS IN THE ROUTINE

—or—

Experience excitement

> *You could not step twice into the same river; for other waters are ever flowing on to you.*
>
> —Heraclitus

No activity, no matter how routine, can be performed in exactly the same way twice. By remembering that each moment is unique, that it has never existed before and will never exist again, I can infuse my life with significance and interest. A child experiences excitement in the most mundane activities—taking a walk, seeing a dog, touching a piece of cloth, breaking bread. How can I learn to see the exciting and the fascinating in my day-to-day? How can I experience my life in the way a child does? How can I step into the same river and recognize its novelty?[56]

ELIAV IS MY THREE-YEAR-OLD son. Yesterday, he and I took a walk to our neighborhood playground that is half a mile away from our home. Even though we have taken the same path dozens of times, it was as if we were walking this route for the first time.

We had no sooner left our house than he shouted, "Dog!!! Daddy, look, it's a dog." It was a neighbor's dog that he had seen dozens of times before, but Eliav didn't allow this fact to dampen his enthusiasm. Next, he saw a car. "Car!!!" he shouted, with the excitement my great-grandparents must have felt when they saw a car for the first time on the dirt roads in their village. And then the sound of the plane flying thousands of feet above us—a sound I had not heard until Eliav pointed it out—reminded him that he, too, not unlike the Wright Brothers or Charles Lindbergh, had defied gravity. Dozens of fresh discoveries were made until we arrived at the playground, where he suddenly saw his friend Omri, whom he had seen an hour earlier in daycare, and they both laughed and hugged as if they had not seen each other in decades, quickly running to the slides together celebrating this special moment.

We cannot live our life the way three-year-olds do, in a constant state of wonderment. It would be too time consuming and exhausting to become entranced with every animal, car, or flying object we encounter, and somewhat awkward if we should embrace a coworker we had seen an hour earlier, with the excitement we greet a long-lost friend. But if we learn again to observe the world through the fresh eyes of a child, we can turn a routine walk into an exciting journey.

Can you find the novel and the exciting in the routine? What can you learn from the way a child experiences the world?

57.

FIGHT THE STORM

—or—

Observe the storm

> *Mindfulness means seeing things as they are, without trying to change them. The point is to dissolve our reactions to disturbing emotions, being careful not to reject the emotion itself.*
>
> —Tara Bennett-Goleman

We all go through rough storms—tough experiences or difficult periods—in our life, and while we can choose to fight the storm, there is another approach we can take, one that is especially useful when dealing with emotional pain. We can simply observe.

For thousands of years, meditators from the East have been practicing the art and science of nonattachment meditation. Just as a fish can look at a furious storm from the calm depth below without becoming entangled in it, so can we train our mind to take a metaphorical step back and merely watch the passionate storm raging within. In most situations, most of us can observe our own dramas in the same way that we observe a drama unfolding onstage—with compassion and curiosity. In the words of psychiatrist Jeffrey Schwartz, “In each moment of your life you are choosing whether to be mindful or not.”[57]

THERE IS AN AFRICAN fable about a hippopotamus that, while crossing a river, lost one of his eyes. Frantically, the hippopotamus began to look for it. He looked for it behind him, ahead of him, on both sides, underneath, but to no avail.

From the bank of the river, the river birds and other animals suggested that the hippopotamus take some time off to rest and recover, but he refused, fearing that he would never find his eye again. And so he continued desperately searching without success, until he was so tired that he had to take a break.

As soon as he stopped moving and calmed down, the river calmed down as well. The mud he had stirred sank to the bottom, and the water became still and clear and transparent. And there, resting on the bottom of the river, he saw his eye.

It is often when we stop and take a step back that we can see clearly through the storm. It is sometimes by doing nothing, by letting go rather than trying to do something, that difficulties pass and problems are resolved.

Are there times when you can simply let the mud sink? Are there places in your life where, rather than creating a stir, you can benefit by observing quietly?

58.

BE UNFORGIVING AND HARSH TOWARD YOURSELF

—or—

Treat yourself with kindness and generosity

> *The more you extend kindness to yourself, the more it will become your automatic response to others.*
>
> —Wayne Dyer

The Golden Rule tells us to not to do unto others what we would not do to ourselves. This assumes that we treat ourselves well, which is not always the case. We are often less forgiving, less generous to ourselves than we are to others. Why is it that so often we treat ourselves worse than we treat others? We do not chastise our friends each time their performance is less-than-perfect, or be harsh on our children whenever they make a mistake—rather we do what we can to comfort and support them. We can bring the same capacity for compassion to our relationship with ourselves. It is out of soft, well-nurtured soil that a seed can grow and flourish.[58]

IN THE YEAR 2000, the eighth Mind and Life Conference was held in Dharamsala, India, attended by some of the leading neuroscientists, as well as by some of the leading Buddhist scholars and practitioners, including the Dalai Lama.

Daniel Goleman, in his book *Destructive Emotions,* captures some of the fascinating discussions that took place during the five days when East met West. One particular exchange revolved around the idea of compassion. The Tibetans were amazed to find out that in Western tradition, compassion is only applied to others—an altruistic emotion—and the Dalai Lama pointed out that *tsewa,* which is Tibetan for "compassion" or "caring," applies to both the self and other people. Love for self and love for others are inseparable, two sides of the same coin. Along similar lines, the Dalai Lama was surprised by the fact that self-love was not universal in the West, and that some people experienced contempt and even loathing toward themselves.

One variation of the Golden Rule—commanding us to love our neighbors as we love ourselves—uses self-love as the standard for loving others and thus presupposes self-love. And yet, throughout the world, entire cultures have been conditioned to consider self-love as something negative, something to be ashamed of. It is time to regain this self-evident, natural right to love yourself.

59.

RUN ON EMPTY

—or—

Fill up

The real enemy of high performance is not stress . . .
the problem is the absence of disciplined,
intermittent recovery.

—JIM LOEHR AND TONY SCHWARTZ

WE GO THROUGH LIFE constantly shifting between emptying and replenishing our energy stores. For instance, we use up resources during the day and then store up energy while sleeping; we expend calories in our various activities and then eat to recover what we've used up. We experience this empty-full cycle also in our emotional and spiritual lives. There are activities that help us recharge our emotional and spiritual batteries (such as listening to the music we like, spending time with loved ones, or taking a vacation) and activities or situations that deplete our energy (such as moments of stress, getting angry, or working around the clock without taking a break).

The empty-full cycle is natural and inevitable. However, in our modern world—where technology has distanced us from our natural cycles—we have to be vigilant about finding the right balance between "fillers" and "emptyers." We do not function at our best when we don't get enough sleep or food, nor when we sleep too much or eat more than we use up; similarly, we will not function at our best psychologically when we are in a state of emotional or spiritual imbalance.[59]

THERE IS A LONG-STANDING debate in psychology between those who believe that our personality is fixed, an immutable part of who we are, and those who believe personality to be malleable, ever changing depending on the situation. Research by Professor Brian Little has gone a long way in reconciling the two seemingly opposite views.

According to Little, we have a "first nature," one that is innate. At the same time, if the situation in which we find ourselves calls for it, we can also act "out of our nature"; that is, in a way that is fundamentally different from our first nature. For example, an introvert in front of an audience can be animated and lively (like an extravert), and an extravert studying for an exam can sit quietly in her room and study (like an introvert).

However, while we are all capable of functioning well out of nature, Little explains that we pay a price for doing so. Acting out of nature drains us; it depletes our energy. This is a problem, unless we learn to balance periods of acting out of nature with periods of acting in accordance with our first nature. For example, an introvert may need time alone following a public lecture, and an extravert may need to party with a large group of friends after an intensive solo study session. Little calls this period of replenishing our energies a “restorative niche.”

This idea of a restorative niche is important, not just to recover after we act out of our nature, but more generally as we go through life expending emotional energies. If we fail to recognize this need, we may end up compensating for our lack of emotional fillers with physical fillers: We may overeat or become addicted to artificial fillers such as coffee or alcohol.

What are your fillers? What activities constitute a restorative niche for you? Refuel, reenergize, regenerate, refill!

60.

SUCCUMB TO FEELING OVERWHELMED

—or—

Think global, act local

Every action of our lives touches on some chord that will vibrate in eternity.

—Edwin Hubbel Chapin

Just open the newspaper or watch the news on TV and it's easy to feel paralyzed, overwhelmed by all the woes of the world. So much work needs to be done that you would be forgiven for feeling that anything that you do is insignificant and pointless.

What has helped me deal with this sense of being overwhelmed, which hits us all from time to time, is the so-called butterfly effect—the idea, which is part of modern chaos theory, is that a seemingly insignificant event can have major consequences (a butterfly flapping its wings on one side of the world can set off a chain of events that results in a tropical storm on the other side of the world). When I first heard of the butterfly effect I felt a great burden lifted off my shoulders. I realized that I could simply be myself and still make a world of difference.[60]

ANCIENT JEWISH TEXTS PROVIDE us with two important ideas to help counter the paralysis that sometimes comes from feeling overwhelmed. In the first, it is written that "whoever saves a life, it is considered as if he saved an entire world." The second says that "you are not obligated to complete the work, but neither are you free to stop doing it." The first idea reminds us of the significance of each person and hence of the importance of our actions no matter how few people we actually affect; the second idea reminds us that we must act regardless of how much else there is to do.

A story from *Chicken Soup for the Soul* captures this ancient wisdom. A man was walking on the beach at low tide, casting back into the ocean starfish that had been washed ashore. A stranger approached him and asked him why he bothered to do what he was doing. After all, there were thousands of starfish on the beach, and on hundreds of other beaches. "Can't you see that you can't possibly make a difference?"

The man looked at the stranger, bent down, picked up another starfish, and threw it back into the ocean. "Made a difference to that one!" he said.

Take some time to think about the causes that are important to you. Commit to action, no matter how small, which will make a difference.

61.

SURRENDER TO NEGATIVITY

—or—

Bring positive energy wherever you go

Wherever you go, no matter what the weather, always bring your own sunshine.

—Anthony D'Angelo

We so often reach the conclusion soon after we wake up that "it's just one of those days," and by doing so create one of those days; or we enter a situation and predict that it's going to be bad—boring, irritating, frustrating, or annoying—and our prediction becomes a self-fulfilling prophecy. In fact, however, we can make most days and most encounters cheerful, lively, positive, and pleasant—if we choose to bring these kind of emotions to the situation. Emotions are contagious. Just as I am affected by other people's moods, other people are affected by mine. If I choose to enter a room with a sense of joy and excitement, my positive mood will spread and will affect those present. And while I should certainly allow myself to experience painful emotions at times, in some situations it may be appropriate to "fake it till I make it" and imbue myself and others with positive energy.[61]

IT WAS ONE OF those mornings. I woke up early to catch a 6 AM flight from Boston's Logan airport on my way to Shanghai. The cab driver taking me to the airport could not stop complaining—first about the Big Dig project in Boston and how it was disrupting traffic and running way over budget, and then about how terrible the government was, and finally about his noisy and impossible neighbor down the street. Now, I'm all for venting and sharing emotions, but this was thirty minutes of nonstop negativity, delivered at 4:30 in the morning when I was half asleep. And I was paying him.

I arrived at the airport in a miserable mood, and then went through security, which didn't help much. I was dreading the next twenty-four hours that I'd be spending in airports and in the air. And then, I saw her. She must have been in her fifties, an airline employee walking off the plane with a food cart. She looked at me, and smiled—a simple, genuine smile. I smiled back, and she said, "I hope you have a wonderful day."

I did, thanks to her. My mood immediately improved. I was even able to laugh about my ride to the airport. Suddenly I was looking forward to my trip again, and to meeting my friends in China.

It may not have been easy for you to smile that morning—it was as early for you as it was for me—and I'm sure you too had good reasons to be in a foul mood. And yet you chose to smile, and you changed my day and the day of many others, I am sure. I want to thank you, though I don't know your name, and I don't even remember what you look like—except for your smile, which I'll never forget.

62.

SUPPRESS

—or—

Express

Holding back our thoughts, feelings, and behaviors can place people at risk for minor and major diseases.

—James Pennebaker

At times we feel afraid to open ourselves up, to express our feelings, to risk seeming weak. The response to our openness may not be what we expect or need. To open up is to take a chance and risk getting hurt. But to choose to remain closed up is not a risk, but a guarantee of loss—loss of intimacy, loss of personal and interpersonal growth, loss of opportunities. And if the risk of opening up is daunting, we can start by taking small steps. We can begin, for example, by opening up to ourselves in a journal, and then, gradually, to those we are close to. Life becomes so much richer, lighter, and more buoyant, when we no longer hold on to the pretense of invulnerability.[62]

IN THE FIELD OF medicine, the link between the mind and the body has been well established—from the placebo effect to the evidence tying stress and suppression with physical aches and pains. According to Dr. John Sarno, a professor at New York University School of Medicine, back pain, carpal tunnel syndrome, headaches, and other symptoms are often "a response to the need to keep those terrible, antisocial, unkind, childish, angry, selfish feelings . . . from becoming conscious." Because physical pain carries less of a stigma in our culture than does emotional disease, our subconscious mind diverts attention—our own and others'—from the emotional to the physical.

The medical advice that Dr. Sarno offers to thousands of his patients is to express rather than suppress: to acknowledge their negative feelings and to accept their anxiety, anger, fear, jealousy, or confusion. In many cases, the mere expression of one's emotions not only makes the physical symptom go away, it alleviates the negative feelings as well.

Psychotherapy works because the client allows emotions—painful and pleasurable—to flow freely. For similar reasons, speaking to a close friend or writing in our journal about our feelings helps us feel better.

Find channels through which you can express your feelings. Open up by writing in a journal or by sharing with a friend, and release some cooped-up emotions.

63.

TIE YOURSELF TO YOUR PAST

—or—

Create your future

> *Nothing is predestined: The obstacles of your past can become the gateways that lead to new beginnings.*
>
> —Ralph Blum

We have no control over our past. We may have had to endure the hardship of a harsh and toxic upbringing, or enjoyed the privilege of a loving and caring family; we may have had the good fortune of a few lucky breaks or the misfortune of some unlucky incidents. But while we cannot change history, we can chart the future. It is certainly true that past experiences dictate, to some extent, our present and future behavior; however, the past's impact is probabilistic rather than deterministic. In other words, through self-awareness coupled with conscious effort, we have the ability to create a life that we want to live. At every moment, the choice whether to be governed by past misfortunes or to steer our life in the direction we desire is ours.[63]

A COMMON STORY IN psychology textbooks describes a pair of identical twins who were raised in a harsh environment, with a father who was often drunk or drugged and who abused them and their mother. When the twins were in their thirties, a psychologist interviewed them both as part of a study.

The first twin that he met was a drug addict living on welfare; his wife and kids had left him after he had abused them for years. In a rare moment when the twin was not drugged or in a rage, the psychologist asked him, "Why are you doing this to yourself and to your family? The twin answered, "How could I have done anything else, given the family I came from?"

The psychologist shrugged, and went to meet the other twin—who was a successful businessman, happily married, and a wonderful parent. The psychologist asked him how he had accomplished all that, to which the twin responded, "How could I have done anything else, given the family I came from?"

The twins were dealt a very similar hand—the same abusive environment, and even the same genes—but they did very different things with it. The first twin resigned to reenacting his past, becoming a slave to it; the second twin chose a different path and created a better future.

What choices do you need to make to create a better future for yourself?

64.

BE CYNICAL

—or—

Be open and sincere

> *Cynicism masquerades as wisdom, but it is the farthest thing from it. Because cynics don't learn anything. Because cynicism is a self-imposed blindness, a rejection of the world because we are afraid it will hurt us or disappoint us.*
>
> —Stephen Colbert

Cynicism is a defense mechanism with which we protect ourselves from being hurt. In fact, however, cynicism does a great deal more damage than good. It exacts a very high price from us, because it drives a wedge between us and others.

It takes a great deal of courage to be sincere and open, for when we pull down our defenses, we become more vulnerable and therefore more likely to be hurt. But this risk is worth taking, as it provides the space for us to create intimacy and joy. Cynicism takes beauty and turns it into the mundane; sincerity takes the mundane and makes it beautiful.[64]

ARISTOTLE, THE ANCIENT GREEK philosopher, said that fiction is more important than history because, whereas history depicts things as they were, fiction shows things as they can and ought to be. The great works of the Renaissance paved the way to a new and better world by providing human kind with a vision of what was possible; the work of the great Romantic artists—such as Beethoven and George Eliot—showed us how high the human spirit could rise.

Film, one of the most important art forms of our age, is also, of course, a very popular one. And popular films often depict for us what is possible in human relations. There is the undiluted romance of *Sleepless in Seattle* and *Casablanca,* the pure positivity of *Pollyanna* and *You Can't Take It with You,* and the unapologetic idealism of *Pay It Forward* and *Dead Poets Society.* Many people dismiss these movies as unreal and naive, but many more watch them and enjoy them. Why? Because we all have a part of us that yearns for the kind of world and the kind of human contact that these movies suggest exist. Under the cynical veneer of the most sophisticated and worldly person beats a sensitive heart that longs for authenticity, hope, and connection.

Why not let down your guard and begin to open up? Why not live with a little more sincerity and a little less cynicism? And if you need some inspiration or guidance, invite your friends over and watch one of those great movies that depict life as it can and ought to be.

65.

ACT HASTILY

—or—

Slow down

Life is too short to be in a hurry.

—Henry David Thoreau

When people compromise on their values—thoughtlessly committing an immoral act or forgoing personal fulfillment in their career because of social pressure—we usually see it as an indication of lack of character. Sometimes, however, the cause is much more benign: the lack of time. Acting swiftly can certainly be beneficial, even necessary. But in our modern world, we've accelerated the pace of life to an unhealthy extreme, forgetting that sometimes slower is better. When we don't take time to think about our actions or deliberate over the choices that we're making, we react to the most immediate and salient source of influence. As a result, we often find in retrospect that we have reacted to social pressures, instead of acting in accordance with our core values.

One of the most effective ways to enhance the likelihood that we will act in accordance with our core values—a key element in living the life we really want to be living—is to slow down and think about what we are really doing and about the implications of our actions.[65]

JOHN DARLEY AND DANIEL BATSON, two psychologists from Princeton University, designed an experiment that resembled the biblical parable of the Good Samaritan. Darley and Batson randomly divided the participants, all Princeton seminary students, into two groups. The first group was asked to prepare a sermon on the Good Samaritan parable; the second group was asked to prepare a talk on another biblical topic. All students received their instructions in one building, and were then asked to walk over to another building where an audience was waiting to hear their sermon.

Before they were sent to give their talk, half of the seminarians were told, "It will be a few more minutes before they're ready for you, but you might as well head on over." The rest of the students were told, "Oh, you're late. They were expecting you a few minutes ago . . . so you'd better hurry." On their way to give their presentations, each student encountered a person who was bent over and appeared to be in pain, feigning sickness and distress. The students had no idea that the person was really an actor, and that they were participating in an experiment.

The outcome was that about two thirds of those who were told they had time stopped to help the person in distress, whereas only a tenth of those who thought they were late did so. These results were not affected by whether their sermon was on the Good Samaritan, or by how devout they were (which was separately measured by the researchers). When the seminarians were later debriefed about the experiment, they were horrified by their own behavior—behavior that did not reflect their core beliefs. It was the pressure they felt—that they had no time, that they had obligations that took precedence over everything else—that led them to behave as they did.

Even in our fast-paced world, take your time to think so that you can make better choices—choices that are in line with your core beliefs.

66.

REMAIN IN YOUR COMFORT ZONE

—*or*—

Stretch yourself

To dare is to lose one's footing momentarily. Not to dare, is to lose oneself.

—Søren Kierkegaard

To venture outside my comfort zone is . . . uncomfortable. To put myself on the line and risk failure is not easy; to fail more often, which is the natural outcome of taking more risks, is never pleasant. However, not trying so that I can avoid failure turns out to be a lot more damaging to my long-term success and overall well-being, than is putting myself on the line and failing. When I dare, when I stretch myself, I am much more likely to fail—and there is certainly a price tag on that—but the cost of not daring and not failing is a great deal higher.[66]

EARLY IN HIS CAREER, Jim Burke, the highly successful CEO of Johnson & Johnson, learned the importance of taking risks from the organization's legendary chairman, General Johnson.

After Burke arrived at Johnson & Johnson he marketed several over-the-counter medications for children. All the products failed miserably. He was called into General Johnson's office, expecting to be fired. Instead, General Johnson extended his hand and said, "I just want to congratulate you. All business is making decisions, and if you don't make decisions you won't have any failures. The hardest job I have is getting people to make decisions. If you make the same decision wrong again, I'll fire you. But I hope you'll make a lot of others, and that you'll understand there are going to be more failures than successes."

General Johnson encouraged his employees to go beyond the safety of the familiar and the certain, and to take risks. Burke embraced this philosophy when he became CEO: "We don't grow unless we take risks. Any successful company is riddled with failures." Burke was named by *Fortune* magazine as one of the greatest CEOs of all time. He had learned, early in his career, that to succeed one must take risks, venture out of the comfort zone and into the stretch zone.

Where in your life are you afraid to exit the comfort zone? Is this fear keeping you back? Stretch yourself.

67.

RESIGN TO THE IMAGE YOU HAVE OF YOURSELF

—or—

Become who you want to be

> *Self-concept is destiny.*
> —Nathaniel Branden

We all have an image of the way we are or the way we believe we ought to be. This self-concept may exert a positive influence on us, but it can also hurt us. The self-concept often assumes the form of a few sentences that describe character traits that we think we have, or certain actions that we must or must not take. For example, my self-concept might contain some of the following: "I am intelligent," "I am attractive," "I have empathy." Alternatively, it might include some of the following limiting beliefs: "I don't deserve happiness," "I must be perfect," "I can't do math," "I am worthless." The image, whether positive or negative, may have its origin in a message we received as children from an adult who played a significant role in our life, or from an experience we had, or even from a deeply embedded cultural norm.

Our self-concept impacts the way we think about ourselves and the world, the way we behave, and the way we experience our life as a whole. And yet, despite the significant impact that our image has on everything that we do, it can be modified. We can plant new messages that we deem more beneficial and that will, over time, replace the old ones. To do so, we need to combine thinking and doing. With persistence—by repeating certain messages *and* aligning our behavior with these messages—we can change the way we perceive ourselves.[67]

ONE OF THE MOST useful self-help exercises that I carry out involves reading a list of characteristics that, for me, capture the way I want to think about myself and the way I want to be.

I came up with this exercise after realizing that the internal voice I often heard in my mind that created my self-concept was not always sympathetic or helpful. For example, the combination of "I am not good enough" and "I am not allowed to make mistakes" was at the core of my struggle with perfectionism. Once I became aware of the cost that messages such as these were exacting from me, I decided to replace them with more helpful ones, such as "I give myself the permission to be human" and "I play and am playful." These may not be relevant or useful to others, but they are deeply meaningful to me.

And so I put together a list of eight affirming messages that I want as my guide to a better life. Each morning I go over my list, spending half a minute or so on each message, thinking about what the message means to me, imagining and feeling what it is like to be the way that I want to be.

Negative messages do not necessarily go away, but over time, as we persist with alternative messages, they lose their centrality and their overwhelming power and have less influence on us.

Rather than reacting to an image that you inherited, create your image and your destiny.

68.

AVOID CHALLENGES

—or—

Commit to overcoming hurdles

> *Commitment unlocks the doors of imagination, allows vision, and gives us the right stuff to turn our dream into reality.*
>
> —James Womack

My life is a journey. I am walking, knapsack on my back, making good progress. Sooner or later, inevitably, I reach a brick wall that stands in the way of reaching my destination. What do I do at this moment? I can choose to take the easy path, turn around, and avoid the challenge posed by the barrier. Or I can throw my knapsack over the wall, thus committing myself to finding ways of getting through, underneath, around, or over it. Declaring that I will reach a certain destination, making a pledge, is about metaphorically throwing my knapsack over the brick wall.

I create my future by expressing, in words and deeds, my commitment to it. Although making a verbal commitment, no matter how bold and how inspiring, does not ensure that I reach my destination, it does enhance the likelihood of success. Words create worlds; acts of courage break barriers.[68]

ON SEPTEMBER 12, 1962, in a speech delivered at Rice University, President John F. Kennedy announced that the United States would land a man on the moon by the end of the decade. At that time numerous barriers stood in the way of such an expedition—much of the needed technology had not yet been invented—but rather than shying away from the challenge, Kennedy committed, throwing the knapsack over the wall.

Kennedy understood the creative, generative power of words. He predicted that this ambitious goal would "serve to mobilize and measure the best of our energies and skills." And he was right. For the next seven years, the levels of motivation and energy within NASA were at an all-time high. Scientists and engineers put their mind and heart toward making Kennedy's words a reality.

On July 20, 1969, Neil Armstrong took one giant step for mankind. Although Kennedy's words were not, in and of themselves, sufficient to achieve the great feat of landing a man on the moon—much hard work from thousands of committed people was necessary—they went a long way to mobilize and motivate those thousands to achieve what only a few years earlier seemed impossible.

Throw your knapsack over the wall. Commit to a goal that is personally important to you, and take a first giant step toward realizing it.

69.

IGNORE THE MUSIC

—or—

Sing, dance, listen

I think I should have no other mortal wants, if I could always have plenty of music. It seems to infuse strength into my limbs and ideas into my brain. Life seems to go on without effort, when I am filled with music.

—George Eliot

According to psychologist Abraham Maslow, dance, rhythm, and music are "excellent ways of moving toward the discovering of identity." In other words, movement and sound can carry us toward our most authentic self, to the place where we are ourselves. In that space, there is no pretense, no facade; in that space there is lightness, simplicity, a genuine state of existence.

The love of music is universal. Most of us have been moved to tears by music and dance—releasing pent-up sorrow or overflowing with joy—and have felt renewed and energized as a result. But for music to have that kind of impact on us, we need to stop running, even if it is merely for a moment or two; we need to devote our attention to it, rather than relegate it to the background. We need to really listen, to absorb the beauty; to move and allow ourselves to be moved.[69]

IMAGINE! IMAGINE LISTENING TO the greatest singers on the planet. Imagine dancing to the music of the greatest composers in history. Imagine singing alongside your favorite performers. For people living barely more than a hundred years ago, this was indeed something to imagine, to dream about. For us, today, right now, this can be a reality.

Until recently, only royalty could afford to have great music played to them at will, and even they did not have as much choice as we do. A king had his private orchestra and possibly a choir that could play and sing for him whenever he wanted. But this form of luxury did not come close to what we have today, with our MP3s and playlists that are the length of a royal decree. We can easily arrange Bach's Brandenburg concertos in our living room, played by the best musicians in the world, or have the Beach Boys join us on our trip to California. We can invite Dvořák to inspire us or Dion to stir us, anytime, night or day. Mozart, Eminem, and Mercedes Sosa are just a click away. Pavarotti's voice can be resurrected and the Pet Shop Boys can reunite—all in our home court—a feat that no court musician or magician could accomplish. The world (of music) is at our fingertips.

What a privilege to live in a world where the best music is easily available to us. Make the most of this gift of modernity! Why not take a five-minute break during the day, when you might need an energy boost, put on your earphones, and listen to your favorite song? Why not turn your car, or the shower, into the Sydney Opera House? Why not transform your living room into the Fabric nightclub, and upon your return home in the evening, embrace a family member or a friend and dance to the sound of music and laughter?

70.

PERCEIVE DIFFICULTY AS A THREAT

—or—

Perceive difficulty as a challenge

> *A pessimist sees the difficulty in every opportunity; an optimist sees the opportunity in every difficulty.*
>
> —Winston Churchill

My words do not merely describe reality, they create reality. If I assess a situation as threatening, I am likely to experience stress. If I assess the same situation as challenging, my emotional reaction is more likely to be one of excitement. The same external event can be experienced very differently, based on the words I use to describe it. Is the upcoming speech a threatening event or a welcomed challenge? What do I tell myself about the rough patch my partner and I are going through right now in our relationship? My reality is a product of both the subjective (my mind) and the objective (what is out there). I am a cocreator of my experiences, of my life.[70]

RESEARCH BY JOE TOMAKA, James Blascovich, and their colleagues illustrates how we can affect our psychological and physiological reaction to a situation by the way we evaluate it. In one study, two groups of students were given the same math test. The first group was told that the task was "difficult mental arithmetic" and were instructed to complete it efficiently and quickly. Not surprisingly, their reaction was to experience the test as *threatening.* The second group were told that the "mental arithmetic" was challenging, and that they should try hard to do their best. Unlike the first group, the second group experienced the test as *challenging.* The second group, those who experienced the situation as a challenge, were calmer, more creative, and actually performed better than members of the first group who evaluated the same situation as a threat.

In other studies, psychologists have documented the physiological effect of how we perceive reality. A single word can make a dramatic difference—in terms of our heart rate, our blood pressure, and other markers associated with stress. Whether we choose to view a situation as a *challenge* or a *threat,* an *opportunity* or a *danger,* a *privilege* or a *menace* can radically influence our overall experience of that situation.

You can evaluate a public lecture that you are about to give as a potential disaster, or as an opportunity to share your knowledge; you can appraise a conflict with your partner as a menace to your relationship or as an opportunity to learn about each other and grow closer; an upcoming meeting with your boss can be perceived as a looming threat or as a welcomed challenge. At least to some extent, how you evaluate—and hence how you experience—situations, is up to you.

71.

AVOID CONFRONTATION AT ALL COSTS

—or—

Be a beautiful enemy

> *He that wrestles with us strengthens our nerves, and sharpens our skill. Our antagonist is our helper.*
>
> —Edmund Burke

In his essay "Friendship," Ralph Waldo Emerson writes that in a friend he is not looking for a "mush of concessions" or "trivial conveniency," for someone who would agree with everything he says. Rather, he is looking for a *beautiful enemy* who will challenge and defy, enhance and elevate him. A person who only wants to be "beautiful" and supportive toward me without ever resisting or confronting does not push me to improve and grow; a person who disputes what I say and do without caring and supporting me is antagonistic and harsh. A true friend must be both beautiful toward me and an enemy.

The idea of a beautiful enemy does not just apply to an intimate relationship with one's friend or partner, but to all relationships—at work and at home. To help other people, we need to have the courage to be honest and forthright, while being empathic and sensitive.[71]

THERE IS A STORY in the Talmud about Reish Lakish, a highway robber, who held up Rabbi Yochanan. The rabbi recognized that Lakish's abilities—his strength, tenacity, persistence, and boldness—could be channeled to learning the Torah and doing good deeds. He convinced Lakish to change his ways, and Lakish became Rabbi Yochanan's student and subsequently his study partner.

The two were beautiful enemies to each other, each challenging and pushing the other to greater and greater heights. Through their work together, they became among the leading scholars of their generation. When Reish Lakish died, Rabbi Yochanan was introduced to a new potential study partner, a great scholar in his own right, but he found him too accommodating, a yes-man. Rabbi Yochanan never recovered from the loss—he sorely missed Reish Lakish's defiance, his incessant questioning and uncompromising search for the truth.

A relationship between beautiful enemies is about transformation. The friends do not just share knowledge, but transform each other—they radically change the way they understand the world and themselves.

Become a beautiful enemy to others, and encourage others to be the same to you. By cultivating a true friendship, you will help each other learn, grow, transform.

72.

SUCCUMB TO FEAR AND INSECURITY

—or—

Be afraid and go ahead anyway

> *Courage is not simply one of the virtues, but the form of every virtue at the testing point.*
>
> —C. S. Lewis

I imagine my heroes, and feel overwhelmed. The undying optimism of Winston Churchill who carried the weight of the free world on his shoulders; the energy and charisma of Anita Roddick who changed the way business is done; the brilliance of Maria Montessori whose insights transformed the field of education. And I sometimes feel insecure about writing the next sentence, or putting together the upcoming lecture. But then, before I surrender and give up, I remind myself that my heroes, too, were sometimes afraid—only they did not allow this feeling to get in their way.

Courage is not about not having fear; courage is about having fear and going ahead anyway.[72]

SELF-PERCEPTION THEORY, PROPOSED BY Cornell psychologist Daryl Bem, suggests that we derive conclusions about ourselves in the same way we derive conclusions about others. For example, if I see a person opening a door for a stranger, I deduce that she's polite; if I see someone screaming at a bystander, I conclude that she is difficult to deal with. In the same way, part of the impression that I form about myself is derived from my observation of my own behavior.

This process applies to the trait of courage. When I see people taking risks, coping with difficulties, or overcoming fear, I infer that they are confident and possess courage. Similarly, if I see myself doing all these things, I infer that I am confident and courageous.

I do not need to *feel* courageous to *act* courageously; rather, it is when I act courageously that I become courageous. Fear is a natural human experience; no one, other than the dead and the psychopath, is entirely free of fear. However, whereas some people succumb to their fear and halt their efforts, others embrace the fear and go ahead anyway.

Where can you embrace your fear and go ahead anyway? Where can you be courageous?

73.

ACT INSENSITIVELY TOWARD OTHERS

—or—

Be nice

Be kind, for everyone you meet is fighting a hard battle.
—John Watson

How I treat others and how I feel about myself are closely connected: The more I treat others with respect, the more I will respect myself; and the more I respect myself, the more I will do the same with others. One of the really nice things about being nice is that it's contagious—when I treat others with respect, they are more likely to treat me in a similar manner, which in turn affects the way I respond, and so on. Our behavior toward other people—colleagues, family members, friends—sends out ripples that impact those we meet, and beyond. Do I choose to spread calm, soothing ripples, or rough and violent waves?[73]

FOR MILLENNIA, GREAT LEADERSHIP has been associated with the crude army general, the tough business leader, the ruthless politician. Our metaphors leave no alternative to this model: After all, in a dog-eat-dog world it's better to be the dog that does the eating than the one that gets eaten; in a Darwinian world, better to be the strongest than the weakest; and to swim in treacherous waters, one has to be a shark.

While there are numerous examples of successful leaders that fit this model, many leaders were no less successful, and achieved their success by being gentle and kind.

Herb Kelleher ran Southwest Airlines for over three decades, making it one of the most successful airlines in aviation history, and among the most admired companies in the world. How? By being very professional—and very nice. Kelleher, of course, had to make tough and unpleasant decisions as the CEO—kindness is no substitute for competence—but he always had in mind the dignity of the people he was dealing with. His humor, generosity, and kindness rippled through his organization, affecting his employees, and through them, the company's customers.

Peter Drucker, the leading management expert of the twentieth century, remarked that manners are the lubricants of the organization. They enable the smooth functioning of organizations—and of relationships in general.

If Kelleher was able to use kindness and generosity to run an incredibly successful enterprise in a very competitive industry, then we can all do so in our daily interactions.

Be kind, be nice, when you meet a customer, a friend, a family member, or a stranger.

74.

BE SOMBER AND GRAVE

—or—

Be playful and light

Remembering what play is all about and making it part of our daily lives is probably the most important factor in being a fulfilled human being.

—Stuart Brown

As children we play a great deal, but then we "mature" and stop having fun. Play, at any age, contributes to our psychological and physical well-being: it makes us more resilient, strengthens our immune system, enhances our creativity, and improves our relationships.

We don't need to restrict play to the leisure activities or hobbies that occupy us once the workday is over. We can choose to bring the spirit of play to a meal with our family or to a road trip with friends, to learning a new skill or to a professional meeting with our colleagues. Fun matters! Regardless of how important and significant our endeavors are, if we go through life with gravity and somberness—without having fun—we will sink into the abyss of meaninglessness and nihilism. Play is our fuel, providing us with energy and drive.[74]

WHEN STUART BROWN, FOUNDER of the National Institute for Play, completed his book, he sent it to me to review. I was deeply moved by the manuscript, and it made me realize just how critical play is for development and growth.

When I finished reading the book, I called my friend Shirley Yuval-Yair and told her that I didn't think my son David was playing enough. There was a moment of silence, and then she said, "Do *you* play enough?" Her words shocked me. She was right. I, too, wasn't playing enough.

Not only was I paying a high price for not playing, but so was David, who was following in my footsteps—because children do what we do much more than what we say. Until that point, play had never been a high priority for me, because who has time to play when there are so many goals and objectives, so much desire and ambition? But Brown's book, coupled with Shirley's question, helped me shift my priorities. And though I still work hard, I have introduced more play into my life—kicking the ball around in our backyard, going on leisurely walks, watching more movies and listening to more music, inviting friends over more often, and for the first time in a long time, reading books that have no direct benefit to my work. My children play more, too.

We talk so much about the importance of quality time, we try so much to squeeze every ounce of productivity and benefit out of every moment of the day. But we forget that regardless of our age, play has to be a priority. As Brown says, "We are built to play, and built through play."

Do you play enough? Bring play and the spirit of play to your work, your relationships, your life.

75.

FOCUS ONLY ON THE IMMEDIATE

—or—

Take the larger context into consideration

> *We tend to focus on snapshots of isolated parts of the system, and wonder why our deepest problems never seem to get solved.*
>
> —Peter Senge

RATIONALITY IS ABOUT BROADENING my horizon and seeing beyond the here and now. When deciding on the appropriate action, I ought to consider the impact of my behavior beyond my immediate surrounding (the here); when making decisions I should be able to look beyond the present (the now) and integrate lessons from the past and projections of the future. The "there and then" informs, and merges with, the "here and now."

I can experience life more fully when I am able to willingly shift perspective and choose when to immerse myself in the present, and when to take a step back and reflect; when to surrender to the here and now, and when rising above the immediate situation is appropriate.[75]

IMAGINE THE FOLLOWING SCENARIO: On your way back from an outing late one night you hear screams from an adjacent street. You run toward the commotion and see a big guy beating up a little guy. The poor little fellow is screaming in agony, and when he sees you he pleads for help. Mustering all your courage, you overpower the brute and free the little fellow, who thanks you and runs off. As you wait for the police to arrest the bully, you feel good about yourself for promoting justice and fairness.

When the police arrive, however, you discover that the little fellow is a fugitive thief; the person you turned in to the police caught the little guy red handed in the middle of a bank robbery. Years go by before the police catch the poor little criminal, during which he continues to steal and pillage.

Our emotions respond to the most salient piece of information available to us at the time, which is why they are sometimes misleading. If one of these pieces is particularly evocative, it will affect our emotions more than will information that may be more significant but less conspicuous. Our rational faculty can provide us with an antidote to the narrow emotional perspective, allowing us to look beyond our spontaneous reaction to a situation and to take into consideration the full context, past and present, before making a decision.

The mistake that the imaginary scenario describes is understandable: The information available was misleading, and there was no time for a Q&A session with the two men. However, many of us unintentionally make a similar mistake—commit a crime of passion—when the entire context is readily available.

When possible, take a step back so that you can look beyond the immediate. Evaluate the situation rationally and pick the most appropriate course of action.

76.

FOLLOW THE PRESCRIBED PATH

—or—

Be the scribe of your own journey

It is easy in the world to live after the world's opinion; it is easy in solitude to live after our own; but the great man is he who in the midst of the crowd keeps with perfect sweetness the independence of solitude.

—Ralph Waldo Emerson

There are two parts to me: the public and the private. One follows the voice of the crowd, the other heeds my internal voice. Other people's opinions are important. They can help me solve problems; they can give me valuable advice; they can help me identify what I want to do—whether in the next moment or with my life as a whole. These voices and opinions, though, can also get in the way of finding my true calling. It is anything but easy to identify the call of my calling, the voice of my vocation. However, to become the author of my own life, I must express my authentic voice, in my writing, my speech, my action.

Do I have the courage to leave safety behind and chart the road not sanctioned?[76]

ON HER WAY BACK home from work one day, Luma Mufleh took a wrong turn and found herself in Clarkston, a small town on the outskirts of Atlanta, Georgia. Children were kicking sticks and stones around in the street, for lack of anything else to play with. This was a level of poverty Luma had not seen since emigrating from Jordan to the United States. She made a few inquiries and found out that Clarkston was a refugee resettlement town whose population came from war-torn countries such as Sudan, Somalia, Ethiopia, Afghanistan, and Bosnia. A few days later she returned to the town and gave the children in the street a soccer ball.

But that wasn't enough for Luma. She wanted to make a real difference in the children's lives, and so, being a soccer player herself, started to coach them. And when they needed help in school, she helped them academically as well, because there was no one else to do it, as many of the parents couldn't read or write English. In 2006, Luma cofounded an organization, the Fugees Family, through which children who have survived wars are given a real chance in their new home.

Luma's journey started with a wrong turn. She left the safety of the road that had been traveled by many. She took a chance, and is now bringing a chance of a better life to others.

Listen to your internal voice. What is it telling you? Be the scribe of your own journey . . .

77.

FOCUS ON THE NEGATIVE

—or—

Focus on the positive

To different minds, the same world is a hell,
and a heaven.
—Ralph Waldo Emerson

Good and bad things happen to everyone, and it is what I choose to focus on that ultimately determines how happy I am. If I focus on the negative or ignore the positive, I create a reality in which the negative is strengthened and the positive is weakened. But if I decide to focus on the positive, I give it strength and actually create a better reality. Even under the most trying circumstances, there is always some good to be found that I can hold on to. And when things are going well, rather than taking what I have for granted, I can celebrate my good fortune.

Focusing on the positive does not mean being detached from reality and ignoring the problems and challenges that exist in every life. On the contrary, it is all about being realistic—by not ignoring the positive, which is as much part of reality as the negative. At every moment, I can choose where I place my focus and where to direct my attention.[77]

SHARON, A FORMER STUDENT of mine, had been married for ten years when she told me this story. The first two years with her partner were blissful, a true honeymoon. But then things took a turn for the worse. The couple started fighting, and Sharon realized that her partner wasn't Mr. Perfect after all. For the following few years, the relationship was miserable for both of them, and they began to think that it might not last.

But then Sharon remembered that in the class she had taken with me when she was an undergraduate, I had recommended John Gottman's book *The Seven Principles for Making Marriage Work.* She reread it, and was reminded of one of Gottman's ideas—that by focusing on the negatives she saw in her partner she was reinforcing them and bringing these behaviors out even more. Focusing primarily on the negative was part of the problem, not the path toward the solution.

She decided to change her focus and started to actively seek the positive. The results amazed her. Not only did she rediscover the wonderful things about her husband—those things that made her fall in love in the first place—she actually helped bring out more positive behaviors in him. Today, ten years into their relationship, Sharon and her partner still have their ups and downs—as every couple does—but their relationship is a great deal better and continues to improve with time.

Create the foundation upon which a happy relationship—and a happy life—can exist. Bring out the best in yourself and in others by focusing on the positive.

78.

RELY ON WORDS

—or—

Lead with deeds

> *Be the change you want to see in the world.*
> —Mahatma Gandhi

The desire to make a difference, to bring about positive change in those we care about and in the world, is deeply engrained in us. But often we need first to change ourselves, if we are to have any chance of changing others. If we want a happier family, we need to work on our happiness; if we want a more moral workplace, we have to exemplify ethical behavior; if we want passionate students, we have to be passionate teachers. To have a lasting influence—whether as teachers, managers, politicians, or parents—we need to lead by example, cultivating in ourselves the qualities that we want to see in others.[78]

IN THE 1940S, WHEN Gandhi had already established himself as a great spiritual teacher, people from all over India came to seek his advice. One day, a woman came to see him. She had traveled a long distance with her small child, and when she finally got to see Gandhi, she told him that she was concerned that her child was eating too much sugar.

Gandhi nodded in understanding, and then asked the mother to return with her child in a month. A month later, the mother and child appeared again before Gandhi. When the mother complained that the child was still eating too much sugar Gandhi turned to him and said, "Stop eating too much sugar!"

The woman respectfully asked Gandhi why he had waited a month to tell her son something he could have done the first time he saw him. Gandhi said, "A month ago I, too, was eating too much sugar." Whether this is a precise account of what had actually happened or a made-up story, it most certainly captures Gandhi's philosophy, and the way he lived his life.

What change do you want to see in the world? What action do you need to take to be that change?

79.

SEEK VALIDATION

—or—

Seek to be known

> *Intimacy is about letting yourself really be known, including parts that you or your partner don't like.*
>
> —David Schnarch

We are often told that the best way to cultivate healthy intimacy with a close friend, a beloved family member, or a romantic partner is to grant and gain validation. But while validation is important at times, and certainly feels good for the giver and the receiver, the real road to intimacy cannot circumvent the path of self-disclosure. When I open up and share my deepest desires, fears, and dreams, I risk being hurt. But at the same time, I create the opportunity for personal and interpersonal growth. When the focus of a relationship shifts from the desire to be validated to the desire to be known, that is when a deep and meaningful connection is created.[79]

IT IS NO GREAT secret that the raw sexual desire we feel at the beginning of a romantic relationship wanes over time. Even if we are with our dream partner, the initial physical attraction diminishes once the honeymoon phase is over. We do not need research psychologists to tell us that novelty produces higher levels of arousal. Many people use this fact to explain, even justify, infidelity: After all, our nature drives us to seek variety, and remaining with the same partner day after day, year after year, seems an antidote to passion.

Sex therapist David Schnarch begs to differ. In years of clinical work and research, he has actually demonstrated that "cellulite and sexual potential are highly correlated." In other words, sex can be better at fifty than at twenty-five, and better after twenty years together than after twenty days. Schnarch does not dispute that novelty is more physiologically arousing, but the physiological component, he argues, is only part of the equation. Intimacy, he says, is much more important than novelty.

How do we cultivate intimacy? By opening up, by sharing our fears and hopes, our fantasies and dreams, our weaknesses and strengths. As we do so, gradually over time we unravel ourselves to our partner, and to ourselves. In this way, we can spend a lifetime becoming better known, cultivating deeper intimacy, and enjoying a more profound, meaningful, and passionate relationship.

The next time you interact with a person you care about and who cares about you, think about how you can become better known. Open up and create intimacy.

80.

SURRENDER TO BOREDOM

—or—

Find the new in the familiar

The voyage of discovery lies not in finding new landscapes, but in having new eyes.

—Marcel Proust

I experience boredom when I trap myself in a rigid mind-set, seeing the world as static, fixed, unchanging. But the world is never still, and life is constantly in flux. How can I experience the same sense of wonder, the same freshness, which a little boy experiences the first time he steps on the grass or becomes aware of a bird? I can live the true wonder and freshness of each moment by noticing new things—whether I think of an uncommon use for a common object, note an unfamiliar expression in a familiar face, try to look at a political challenge from a different perspective, or search for distinctive details in a musical piece I've heard dozens of times.[80]

WE OFTEN RUN THROUGH our busy days without stopping, mindlessly processing our surroundings in a way that allows us to ignore the world entirely. Not only do we experience boredom as a result, but we also compromise our physical and psychological well-being. As psychologist Ellen Langer has demonstrated, we can exit this state and become mindful with relatively little effort.

Ask yourself the following questions: What do you notice about your surroundings that you have not noticed before? What novelty do you recognize in your partner or children, even though you've been looking at them day after day for years? Can you think of new uses for any of the objects that you see right in front of your eyes right now? Asking yourself these and similar questions on a regular basis and putting some effort into coming up with interesting, exciting, and fun answers induces a state of mindfulness.

Ellen Langer's work over the years illustrates that even a moment or two of living mindfully in this manner—"drawing novel distinctions" whenever and wherever—can promote our physical and mental health. Taking a little time to live mindfully, we strengthen our immune system, enjoy a significant increase in our happiness and energy levels, improve our memory and creativity, and become more accepting of ourselves and others. We also perform better professionally, and our relationships improve. So rather than surrendering to boredom, start asking the questions and turn the *same old* into the *distinctly new.*

81.

LIVE ONLY IN THE MIND

—or—

Experience heartfelt positivity

We think too much and feel too little.

—CHARLIE CHAPLIN

SOCRATES REMARKED THAT "the unexamined life is not worth living." Aristotle described the human being as a "rational animal." They were both right—and yet their view of humankind is incomplete. In addition to being given the capacity to think and examine, we were also endowed with the capacity to feel and experience, and we ignore this side of ourselves at our peril. In the modern world of science and rationality, where supercomputers are the super role models, we often forgo the feeling component of our nature. And while a life of mere whim and emotion cannot fully satisfy a human being, neither can a life of constant evaluation and controlled emotions.

I become whole as I engage my heart through focusing my mind—on the person I love, the rich tastes and smells, the present moment, the life I'm living. I am *also* a "feeling animal," and the unfelt life is not worth living.[81]

PROFESSOR BARBARA FREDRICKSON CONDUCTED a study in which employees in an organization exercised loving kindness meditation at work for twenty minutes each day. During that time, they were encouraged to experience the love they felt toward a close friend, a child, a partner, or themselves.

The effect was astounding, going far beyond the immediate positive feeling that the meditation exercise created in the participants. During the seven weeks of the study (and in some cases long after), participants experienced a decrease in levels of anxiety and depression, an increase in their general feeling of joy and happiness, improved physical health, better relationships, and a higher sense of purpose.

One of the participants describes the effects of the study on her life: "I feel more confident with myself and with people around me. I am not so hard on myself. I have been able to forgive things easier than before. . . . I feel that I grew spiritually. I feel more at peace with myself. I am not as stressed as I was before I began the study. I look at people's personalities differently and empathize with them more."

Fredrickson showed that the benefits in this intervention stemmed from the experience of *heartfelt positivity*: "Positivity was the active ingredient, the engine of change."

Those who spent their time being moved by their favorite music, or experiencing gratitude for the gifts in their life, or savoring a beautiful work of art, or sitting quietly in the woods, enjoyed similar physical and psychological benefits as did those who experienced love and kindness toward others.

Spend more time experiencing positive emotions. You can do it even for a few seconds right now or at every other moment in your life, or you can put aside twenty minutes each day and enjoy the benefits of heartfelt positivity.

82.

GIVE UP WHEN THE GOING GETS TOUGH

—or—

Work toward your dreams

> *If one advances confidently in the direction of his dreams, and endeavors to live the life which he has imagined, he will meet with a success unexpected in common hours.*
>
> —Henry David Thoreau

"There is no substitute for hard work," said Thomas Edison. No mountain was conquered, no meaningful goal was attained, without persistence. When I want to give up, I remind myself that no person is immune to feelings of uncertainty and insecurity—and that all people who have accomplished a significant feat endured difficult times and were lured by the sirens of surrender. But they continued along the road to their destination, and if they did take a break, it was only a temporary one, a much-needed and well-earned rest.

There are moments when I want to put my tools down, give up my aspirations, and drift aimlessly. In such moments I remind myself that the only way to realize my dreams is through persistence, dedication, and hard work.[82]

IN THEIR BOOK *Psychological Capital,* Fred Luthans, Carolyn Youssef, and Bruce Avolio tell the story of Mary, who, as a teenager, lost her mother and had to stay with her abusive father and bitter stepmother. After a few run-ins with the law and her being moved from one foster home to the next, her life seemed to be taking the predetermined path that so many other at-risk children follow. But then something happened. A close friend of hers at school challenged her to assume control over her life. And she chose to do just that.

Mary began to invest her energy in her education and in athletics, and she excelled at both, earning a scholarship to a top college. She continued to put effort into her studies and earned good grades. In addition, she worked hard at whatever job she had, whether as a babysitter doing additional household chores without extra pay, or going beyond the call of duty in her summer internship at a bank. Her conscientiousness and hard work did not remain unnoticed. She was eventually offered a full-time position at a bank, and within a few years became the vice president responsible for marketing and retail. Mary had "a moment that mattered in taking charge of her own life," and in that moment decided that rather than giving up when the going got tough, she would work toward making her dreams a reality.

When the going gets tough for you, get going!

83.

COMPROMISE ON YOUR BEST SELF

—or—

Act from the best within

> *Always be a first-rate version of yourself, instead of a second-rate version of somebody else.*
>
> —Judy Garland

At each juncture, at each crossroad, I have the choice between insisting on my best self and settling for less. How do I respond to my partner's criticism? What do I tell my boss? Do I allow the generous or petty self to reign supreme? Do I lash out in anger or embrace with tenderness? To decide what that best self is, I often have to see myself and the situation from the outside, to take a step back and evaluate dispassionately—which is not always easy, especially when emotions run high, or when external pressure mounts. To find the best within me I can draw on help from the best without by asking myself: What would my role model, the person I admire, do in my situation?[83]

THE SCULPTOR MICHELANGELO WAS asked how he created his most impressive and beautiful masterpiece, the statue *David.* His response was that he went to the quarries at Carrara, found a large block of marble, and in it he saw David. All he then needed to do for David to emerge was remove the excess marble.

Just as beautiful David—or the potential for David—existed within the marble block, so within each of us exists a beautiful self. That self may be hiding as a result of harsh encounters, undercover as a consequence of having been hurt, and yet no matter what, it is always there, ready to be uncovered and expressed.

We do not need to have the genius of Michelangelo to see the potential for beauty in ourselves. We can dedicate ourselves right away to the task of identifying and cultivating the seed of greatness that exists in each of us. To realize the potential within us we need to study our best past and apply it to our present and future.

When were you at your best? What were some of the encounters you had with others that you are most proud of? What are you like when you're at your best? The answers to these questions can provide you the blueprint for creating yourself in the image of your ideal self.

In every encounter, insist on your best self!

84.

OVERLOOK HUMAN POTENTIAL

—or—

See the seed of greatness in each person

> *To see things in the seed, that is genius.*
>
> —LAO-TZU

GREAT LEADERS, BE THEY teachers or managers or parents, are able to see the seed of greatness in themselves and others—to see the potential that lies within every child and adult. In each encounter we can actively seek the seed of greatness that exists in the person in front of us. Simple questions, such as, "What is most impressive and remarkable about him?" or "What are her unique talents and gifts?" can open our eyes to the possibilities that they hold within. When we become aware of their inner seed of greatness, we help them liberate the potential that they possess and may have hitherto overlooked.

A seed, to grow, needs water and light; by recognizing the potential in others, we cultivate their seed of greatness, providing the necessary nourishment for growth and flourishing.[84]

IN THE 1960S, PSYCHOLOGIST Robert Rosenthal and school principal Lenore Jacobson carried out a seminal study in the field of education. Elementary school students were given a standard IQ test, and the results were reported to the teachers. The teachers, however, were misled on two counts. First, they were told that the test was not an IQ test but a test that identified those students who were about to enjoy above-average intellectual progress in the coming year, and thus would significantly improve their academic performance. Second, the list that they were given of those students who supposedly did especially well on the test—those who, in other words, had the highest academic potential—was in fact a random list of names.

At the end of the year, those students who had been randomly labeled "high potential" actually became better students. Their achievements in the humanities as well as in the sciences improved considerably, compared to the rest. Most astonishingly, the IQ of those who were on the random list increased significantly.

The study has been replicated successfully many times all over the world. It has also been replicated in other areas, such as business and the military. Each time, the results confirm the initial conclusion of the study: The expectations of others—be they teachers, parents, managers, or military commanders—significantly impact the performance of their students, employees, and soldiers. To a great extent, we get what we expect of others: Beliefs are self-fulfilling prophecies.

Can you see the seed of greatness in other people? Can you release the potential that lies within them?

85.

UTTER EMPTY WORDS AND PROMISES

—or—

Live with integrity

> *By a lie, a man throws away and, as it were, annihilates his dignity as a man.*
>
> —IMMANUEL KANT

INTEGRITY, ACCORDING TO THE dictionary, is "the quality or condition of being whole or undivided." I have integrity when no separation exists between what I say and what I do, when there is congruence between my words and my actions. My integrity determines, to a great extent, the respect that others have for me and, more important, the respect that I have for myself. When I follow up on my commitments, I send an important message to myself and to others—that my thoughts, my words, and myself matter. My words are an expression of myself, and, therefore, when I honor my words, I am honoring myself.[85]

RESEARCH BY PSYCHOLOGISTS Dafna Eylon and Scott Allison shows that our legacy—what we're remembered for—is determined to a large extent by how moral we are in our lifetime. People who led an upright life—who led a life of integrity—are viewed even more favorably after their death; whereas immoral people are viewed even less favorably after they die, regardless of how successful they were when alive.

Few people enjoy a more positive lasting legacy than the sixteenth president of the United States, Abraham Lincoln. One of the characteristics he is most admired for is his integrity. Honest Abe, as he is sometimes referred to, had in his lifetime a reputation for a "morbid compulsion for honesty."

Before becoming a politician, Lincoln was a lawyer. He once defended a client, only to discover in the middle of the trial that the man was actually guilty. Lincoln turned to his associate, Leonard Swett, and said, "Swett, the man is guilty; you defend him, I can't," and he quit, giving up a large fee. In another trial, the prosecution submitted evidence that, Lincoln believed, implicated his client. Lincoln stood up in the courtroom and left in disgust. When the judge called him to return to the courthouse and continue with the trial, Lincoln refused. He sent a message: "Tell the judge, my hands are dirty; I came over to wash them."

I doubt that Lincoln was thinking about the impact of these acts on his legacy. However, it is clear that Lincoln understood the price he would pay—a price we all pay, whether or not we're conscious of it—for breaches of integrity. Lincoln realized that the cost of leaving a trial midway—awkwardness, money, the prestige of winning—was trivial when compared to the price paid for willful dishonesty.

86.

FLAUNT YOUR FEATHERS

—or—

Be humble

> *Talent is God-given. Be humble.*
> *Fame is man-given. Be grateful.*
> *Conceit is self-given. Be careful.*
> —John Wooden

Whereas arrogance is a sign of insecurity and lack of self-confidence, modesty is the hallmark of a person with high levels of self-esteem. When I respect myself, I am more likely to act with humbleness, for I have no need to elevate myself in the eyes of others to "fix" my wounded sense of self; when I esteem myself, I do not feel compelled to flaunt my successes and put my trophies on display. Being humble is not necessarily about hiding my skills and strengths. It is about being attuned to the situation, sensitive to other people, and recognizing my real abilities as well as my limitations.[86]

THE HASIDIC RABBI SIMCHA BUNIM used to say that we should walk around with two slips of paper in our pocket, one with the words "The world was created for me," and the other with the words "I am but dust and ashes." Together, these slips of paper would help us achieve emotional balance. When we are feeling down, the first would remind us how important we really are; when we are feeling overconfident and invulnerable, the second slip would remind us of our humble origin and ultimate end.

According to psychologist Abraham Maslow, these two reminders are necessary for us to fulfill our potential for personal development and public contribution, because an excess of either self-confidence or insecurity prevents us from growing. If I am arrogant and conceited, I am likely to fall flat on my face, experiencing frustration and disillusionment. If I do not believe in my abilities, I am unlikely to get off the ground.

Maslow wrote of the need for the "graceful integration between the humility and the pride that is absolutely necessary for creative work . . . You must be aware not only of the godlike possibilities within, but also of the existential human limitations."

Imagine that you have these two pieces of paper in your pockets. Remind yourself of their messages so that you can find the healthy balance between humbleness and pride.

87.

TAKE ON MORE AND MORE

—or—

Simplify your life

> *Simplicity, simplicity, simplicity! I say let your affairs be as two or three, and not a hundred or a thousand; instead of a million count half a dozen.*
>
> —Henry David Thoreau

Quantity affects quality; there is such a thing as "too much of a good thing." Even if every individual activity I engage in has the potential to make me happy, if I pile too much on my plate, I can still end up being unhappy with my life. There comes a point at which the additional activity—no matter how wonderful and desirable it might be in itself—adds misery rather than joy.

Our world is becoming more complex and the pressure mounts by the nanosecond. Less can be more: If my life is overburdened, if I am too busy, then cutting down on my activities—simplifying my life—will make me happier, and will boost my creativity, my level of enthusiasm for everything I do, and ultimately, my overall success.[87]

WARREN BENNIS WAS AN MIT professor studying and teaching leadership. He decided to put his ideas on leadership to the test, and agreed to become the president of the University of Cincinnati. His life immediately became busier; his responsibilities piled up, and though he was successful—or, perhaps, *because* of his success at his new job—he had little time left over for pursuing his true passions, which included teaching, writing, and research.

In his seventh year as president, Bennis was invited to give a lecture at Harvard, where a former colleague asked him, "Do you like being a university president?" Bennis, rarely short of words, was stumped. It was only later, after much reflection, that he realized that what he liked was the *idea* of being a university president. He left his position and went back to being a professor, focusing once more on teaching, writing, and research.

Since his departure from the role of a university president, Bennis has enjoyed the most productive and prolific period of his life, publishing some of the most influential books in the area of leadership. His impact on leaders in politics, education, and business is enormous, and he is credited with establishing leadership as an important academic field.

Sometimes we don't have a choice about how busy we are. And when we do have a choice, taking on additional responsibilities may be fine—as long as it is done for the right reasons. The problem is that so many of us pile on more and more activities for the wrong reasons, not because we are passionate or believe in something, but because we are told to, or are expected to, or like the idea of doing so. Consequently, we end up compromising on our productivity, creativity, and happiness.

How can you become less busy? How can you simplify your life? Commit to doing less rather than more.

88.

EXPERIENCE YOUR MISTAKES AS CATASTROPHES

—or—

Treat your mistakes as valuable feedback

Freedom is not worth having if it does not connote freedom to err.
—Mahatma Gandhi

Mistakes and errors are an inescapable part of any life, and a critically important part of a successful life. We learn to walk by falling, to talk by babbling, to shoot a basket by missing, and to color the inside of a square by scribbling outside the box. If we perceive the possibility of mistakes as a catastrophe, we will refrain from trying and fall short of our potential; in contrast, when we see mistakes as feedback, we open ourselves up to the opportunity of learning and growing. Moreover, when we stop obsessing about deviating from the straight and narrow—when failure is no longer our enemy—we experience a lightness of being, free of the oppressive facade of perfection.[88]

IN A POP!TECH PRESENTATION, conductor and teacher Benjamin Zander demonstrated to the audience what it means to be liberated from the fear of failure. In the presentation, Zander is working with a fifteen-year-old cellist, helping him achieve his potential.

At one point, while playing a Bach piece, the young cellist makes a mistake and is visibly upset. When he finishes playing the piece, Zander suggests that instead of agonizing over the mistake, he should say, "How fascinating!" Both the cellist and the audience laugh in relief at no longer having to take failure so seriously. Zander then continues working with the cellist through the piece, and when he makes a mistake again, Zander jubilantly declares, "How fascinating!"

After fifteen minutes of being liberated from the tyranny of the fear of failure, the cellist's playing is transformed. His music is so much lighter, freer, more joyous. Just like life as a whole can be, at each moment, if we begin to see failure for what it is—fascinating feedback.

89.

ENGAGE IN SELF-ANALYSIS

—or—

Focus outward

Individuals whom we describe as self-confident or possessed of self-respect seem to be characterized not so much by a feeling of esteem for themselves as by an absence of concern with themselves.

—David Shapiro

I SUSPECT THAT DEPRESSION is on the rise in large parts of the modern world, at least in part, because self-analysis is encouraged and self-help books are abundant. People are more concerned about their mental health than they were a hundred years ago, and the concern itself may generate discontent: Our obsession with happiness contributes to our unhappiness. While Socrates was right that the unexamined life is not worth living, it is equally right that the overexamined life is tedious and ultimately depressing.

So do we stop with self-analysis and discard self-help? Not at all. We need to find the right balance between our focus on ourselves and our focus on the outside world, between analyzing and doing, between reflecting and acting. So sometimes, instead of worrying about yourself or analyzing your thoughts and feelings, think about what you can do for others; instead of focusing on your problems, go out and make someone else feel better.[89]

I WENT INTO POSITIVE psychology, the science of happiness, because I wanted to find more meaning and pleasure in my life, and I conducted research on self-esteem to build my own self-confidence and self-respect. Over the years I have become healthier psychologically, both happier and with a more robust sense of self. There were times, however, when I felt that my focus on the psychology of happiness contributed to my unhappiness, and that my incessant involvement with the psychology of self-esteem was hurting me more than it was helping.

It took me a few years to realize that my attempt to solve the problem was in fact part of the problem—and I began to, more often, redirect my attention outward. For example, setting a compelling goal helped me focus on something external and hush the constant internal dialogue. For similar reasons, focusing much more on helping others—as a teacher and author—helped. Starting a family significantly contributed to my happiness, at least in part because the *I* relinquished center stage to the *we.*

Despite these internal and external changes that have taken place in my life, like many others I sometimes find myself living the examination more than life itself. And while I recognize that some self-reflection and concern about my psychological state is important—ignoring our needs is not the answer—redirecting my thoughts to another person or to a cause can often help strike a healthier balance.

When you find yourself deep inside yourself, engaged in too much self-analysis, refocus your attention outward.

90.

TAKE YOUR NEARS AND DEARS FOR GRANTED

—or—

Appreciate your family and friends

Friendship doubles joy and cuts grief in half.
—Francis Bacon

The number-one predictor of well-being is not money or prestige, not success or accolades, but rather the time we spend with people we care about and who care about us. And yet, in pursuit of great feats and distant shores, we so often take for granted—fail to appreciate and savor—those near to us. Unfortunately, it often takes a loss or an illness of someone dear, a major disappointment, or some tragedy to remind us of what truly matters. But do we need to wait for something terrible to happen, to truly appreciate the ones we love?

Not only will we be happier if we take the time to enjoy our relationships, through those precious times with those close to us, we will gain the strength to conquer faraway places.[90]

SHIRLEY YUVAL-YAIR IS A therapist, singer, and author. She sees clients during the day, she performs almost every evening, and she publishes children's books. And she is happily married and has three small children.

How does she manage? It's not easy. Often, Shirley finds herself in the evening sitting with her kids around the table, but thinking about her performance later that night and of all the things she needs to take care of before she leaves—such as preparing the children's schoolbags, helping them bathe and brush their teeth, and getting a few minutes to talk to her partner about tomorrow's plans.

Whenever this happens—when she is with her family and yet finds herself distracted, thinking about what needs to get done—she reminds herself that "this is it." These are the good old days, that she does not want to miss twice—when they're gone, and when they're actually happening. She says, "It's as if I have an internal switch that brings me back to the experience, and I appreciate my children, my husband, being together with the people I love so much."

The essence, the primary source of life's ultimate currency, is the baths that elicit hearty laughter and passionate shrieks, the deep conversation with our best friend, the nurturing kiss with our partner grabbed in between everything else.

So once in a while, as you're frantically getting things done at work, or face dozens of chores at home, or right now, remember what truly matters in life.

91.

EXPERIENCE INSIGNIFICANCE

—or—

Lead a spiritual existence

> *At any moment, you have a choice, that either leads you closer to your spirit or further away from it.*
>
> —Thích Nhất Hạnh

We are body and mind, flesh and spirit—and everything that we do in our life reflects this duality. What we do in each moment—whether at work or spending time with a best friend—can be perceived as either predominantly physical or spiritual.

The *Oxford English Dictionary* defines spirituality as "the real sense of significance of something." I often refer to this definition in my work, as it provides a reminder that we can choose to focus on the real significance in what we do (such as connection to people or the contribution of our action) or to become hostage to the deceptive glitter masquerading as significant (such as material possessions or accolades). When we recognize and remind ourselves of the truly significant in that which we do, we can begin to turn our life into a spiritual journey. Moreover, when we remind ourselves that what we do in a specific moment matters, matter and spirit become one.[91]

PERHAPS NO DOMAIN IS situated further away from spirituality in people's mind than business. However, an increasing body of research points to the importance of spirituality for the success of an organization—be it a school or a bank, a soup kitchen or a management consulting firm. In his work on spiritual leadership, Professor Louis Fry shows that introducing a spiritual component to the way an organization runs is critical for motivating managers and staff.

It is relatively easy to think about priests and rabbis introducing spirituality in their congregation, and with little effort we can imagine medical practitioners or teachers infusing their work with the transcendent and sacred. However, how does one introduce spirituality to fields such as banking or consulting or law? Fry convincingly argues that leaders, regardless of their organization or industry, need to clarify their values, to communicate these values through a vision, and take action that fits in with these values.

This is true not only for organizations but for individuals as well. What are *your* core values? What matters most to *you* in the work that you do, beyond the material rewards it offers? Is it integrity? Giving? Excellence? Is it being kind? Once you identify your values, you may want to draw up a short list that you can keep with you at all times and use as a reminder of what matters most to you. And then do your best to live in accordance with your values.

Live your vision and turn your life into a spiritual journey!

92.

BLINDLY FOLLOW

—or—

Lead!

> *The follower who is willing to speak out shows precisely the kind of initiative that leadership is made of.*
>
> —Warren Bennis

History is full of examples of ordinary individuals who followed charismatic leaders and went on to commit horrendous acts of violence. Whether it's Hitler leading his followers to commit genocide, or Jim Jones leading his followers to mass suicide, these and other leaders exploited a natural and common inclination most of us have: to follow. Inherent in the desire to follow is the desire to be told what is right and wrong.

In numerous experiments, psychologists have highlighted the human inclination to obey a charismatic figure, to conform to the will of the majority, or even to do nothing in the hope that others will act instead of us. But we can choose not to follow blindly, not to conform unthinkingly. We can choose to open our eyes, think for ourselves, and take action where we know that action is necessary. And while, at times, following others may be the right thing to do, we have the responsibility to decide when it is appropriate to do so and when we ought to take the lead.[92]

IN THE 1950S, WHEN Joseph Stalin was the premier of the Soviet Union, Nikita Khrushchev was the leader of the Communist Party. After Stalin's death, Khrushchev visited the United States and met reporters at the Washington Press Club.

Following a brief presentation, participants asked him questions, verbally and in writing. One of the written questions he was asked was, "Today you talked about the hideous rule of your predecessor, Stalin. You were one of his closest aides and colleagues during those years. What were you doing all that time?"

Khrushchev paused and looked at the audience. His face grew red and he became visibly angry. He took a deep breath and then shouted to the audience, "Who asked that question?" A few seconds went by, and once again he screamed, "Who asked that?" No one responded, and there was complete silence in the press club. A few long seconds later, Khrushchev said quietly, "That's what I was doing."

There was no threat of a gulag in Washington, Khrushchev had no way of hurting anyone who attended the event, and yet the reporter who asked the question was afraid to stand up and take responsibility for his words.

It is not easy to stand up and lead, especially when there is a price—social, material, or other—to pay for the act of leadership. We, too, often tend to conform, to rationalize our inaction, to look the other way.

This is why there are so few whistleblowers who are prepared to reveal corruption, so few brave individuals who have the courage to swim against the current, and so few real leaders who are willing to take responsibility.

If you want a better, more moral and just world, you must lead, whether you're onstage or in the audience.

93.

BE HARD ON THE PERSON

—or—

Be hard on the problem

> *Once you separate the person from the problem you can both team up and attack the problem together, instead of attacking each other.*
>
> —Marelisa Fábrega

An unpleasant fact of life is that we sometimes need to say difficult things that others may not want to hear. We may need to reprimand our children, or point out the failings of employees, or express our unhappiness at something our partner did. These encounters are never easy—neither for the person communicating the message nor for the one receiving it. In such situations, psychologist Haim Ginott recommends, it is important to separate the person from the behavior. Be as harsh as you need to be when dealing with the problem, but as soft as you can with the person.

While it's impossible to entirely eliminate the unpleasant feelings involved in every exchange, it is possible to minimize them, and equally important, to enhance the likelihood that some good will come out of the exchange.[93]

BILL DOYLE WAS MY squash coach at Harvard. During my freshman year I was not committed to the team. For me, training felt like a burden; it was something I had to do rather than something I wanted to do. I was one of the top college players in the country, so I knew that the team needed me and that my place on the team was not in danger. Still, I felt increasingly frustrated by the situation, and I knew that Bill and the other players felt uncomfortable with my behavior.

About halfway through the season, Bill told me that he wanted to have a talk. This was no surprise, and I went in to see him, expecting to have a heated exchange with him, after which I would storm out of the room, never to play for the squash team again.

But Bill had other ideas.

He started by saying, "Tal, the players and I really want you on the team, but not at the price of the team." He explained to me that my behavior hurt team morale and was unfair toward other team members. In a quiet and pleasant yet assertive voice, he told me that I had a choice: "You're either on the team with all that that entails in terms of privileges and obligations, or you're off the team. I will respect any decision you make."

This was not what I had expected. I told Bill that I would think about it. A few hours later, I told him that I wanted in.

Being part of the squash team for the next three years turned out to be my most meaningful experience at Harvard. Even today, some of my best friends are former teammates. I learned from Bill important lessons about being part of a team and about leading by separating the person from the behavior.

94.

BE A PASSIVE VICTIM

—or—

Be an active agent

> *Having a strong sense of controlling one's life is a more dependable predictor of positive feelings of well-being than any of the objective conditions of life we have considered.*
>
> —Angus Campbell

I can go through life as a victim, blaming others for my misfortunes, and experiencing frustration over my condition. Or I can choose to be an active agent and do what I can do to bring about a positive change in my life. I can go through life complaining about my parents, my boss, my partner, my health, my finances, my overall bad luck, or I can take these and other circumstances and shape them into the life that I want.

We're quite good at making excuses—justifying inaction or wrong action. It is often easier to find reasons why nothing needs to be done than to step up to the plate, and to blame others rather than to admit that we've erred. The antidote to making excuses is taking responsibility. Instead of using our mental energy to find excuses, instead of spending our limited resources rationalizing and justifying what we did or did not do, we ought to focus our efforts on learning from the past and creating a better future. A can-do attitude—taking initiative rather than being resigned to one's circumstances, making things happen rather than waiting for them to somehow occur—is one of the most significant predictors of success and happiness.[94]

ACCORDING TO PSYCHOLOGIST Nathaniel Branden, considered the father of the self-esteem movement, taking responsibility is one of the pillars of a healthy sense of self. Branden goes on to explain that we internalize the idea of taking responsibility as soon as we truly accept the fact that "no one is coming." No princess bride or knight in shining armor is coming to rescue me from the situation I am in; no sage or teacher is coming to reveal the truth and show me the light; no boss is coming to recognize and reward my true potential and lead me to the promised post. When I realize that making a positive difference in my situation (and even in the world) is up to me, and me alone, I am ready to take responsibility and make the most of my life.

Branden was discussing this idea in a workshop, when one of the participants challenged him. The participant told Branden that he understood the importance of taking responsibility, but then added that he didn't agree with the statement that no one is coming. "How do you mean?"

asked Branden, to which the participant responded, "It's not true that no one is coming because, Dr. Branden, you came!"

Branden paused for a few seconds, and then responded, "You are right, I came. But I came to tell you that no one is coming!"

Are there areas in your life where you are blaming, complaining, and making excuses, waiting for something to somehow happen? Stop waiting, take responsibility, and make things happen.

95.

REMAIN STUCK

—or—

Change your perspective

Maybe the art of life is to convert tough times to great experiences: We can choose to hate the rain or dance in it.

—Joan Marques

Sometimes simply changing perspective and looking at a difficult situation differently can help us overcome the feeling that we are stuck. We can look at a situation that elicits the feeling of threat as challenging and experience a very different reaction to it; we can change our perspective about a person who usually annoys us, and by actively looking for the good begin to enjoy our interactions; we can see a failure as a learning opportunity thus putting ourselves in a much better position to bounce back; and at times we have the choice to find a deep sense of meaning in a painful situation and turn it into a growth experience.

While the objective circumstances matter a great deal, no less important is our subjective interpretation of the situation—the way we (the subject) perceive the situation (the object).[95]

IN ONE OF THE most memorable moments in film, Keating, the unconventional teacher in *Dead Poets Society*, gets on the desk in the middle of class and declares, "I stand upon this desk to remind myself that we must constantly look at things in a different way. . . . You see, the world looks very different from up here." His students are shocked by his unexpected behavior, but Keating does not end his lesson there, and helps the students to experience the shift in perspective themselves. He gets them to stand on their desk, too, and when some of them are ready to jump back down on the ground, he says, "Now, don't just walk off the edge like lemmings! Look around you!"

Through his words and deeds Keating gets his students to look at things from a new perspective. By breaking norms of behavior, he presents an alternative way of seeing and being.

When we find ourselves in a tough spot, we need to remind ourselves that there is usually an alternative way of looking at the situation. Shifting our perspective is the first step to changing our reality.

My ability to change perspective does not mean that I can always choose to take on the easy or pleasant route; sometimes facing difficulties head on, with all that that entails, is the right thing to do. However, I can often avoid unnecessary hardship and pain by taking a different perspective, by seeing the same person, experience, or object in a different light, through a different lens.

When you're feeling stuck, try changing your perspective. It may help to get on the table and look around . . .

96.

DWELL ON FAILURES

—or—

Focus on successes

> *Where your attention goes, your energy flows and life grows.*
>
> —Brian Bacon

Learning from failure is important; all successful people and organizations do so. But many people dwell too much on their failures, without giving their achievements and successes their due. This distorted view of reality—seeing the negative and ignoring the positive—leads not only to unhappiness, but also to suboptimal performance.

Learning from what worked is no less important than learning from what did not; past failures can guide us in terms of what we should not do, past successes can guide us toward what we can and ought to do more of. When we remember our successes, we become inspired and energized, and thus better prepared emotionally to take on new challenges. [96]

IN THEIR BOOK *Appreciative Coaching,* Sara Orem, Jacqueline Binkert, and Ann Clancy tell the story of Patty, a woman in her sixties who wanted to run her own part-time business as a mortgage loan officer. At first, when she began as a junior loan officer, she felt intimidated by her young, computer-savvy, fast-thinking colleagues. It didn't occur to her to consider how valuable her own experience was, which she had gained through a lifetime of building relationships and working with people: "It was as if her strengths and past experiences had been erased from her consciousness."

Patty started working with a coach who helped her highlight her past successes. The more Patty talked about her abilities and strengths—the more she focused on her positive past—the more confident she became about her future. With the increase in her confidence levels, and by exercising her strengths, success promptly followed.

We can bombard ourselves with positive self-talk and positive thinking—telling ourselves that we are capable of doing something, that the sky is the limit, that the future is bright. However, the impact of such words and assurances is unlikely to push us *forward* to a better future, unless we can *back* them up with evidence of a positive past.

Your positive past holds within it the seeds of your future success. Rather than allowing these seeds to be left unnoticed, to wither and die, water them and help them grow.

97.

SUPPRESS YOUR TEARS AND FEARS

—or—

Give yourself permission to be human

> *One's suffering disappears when one lets oneself go, when one yields—even to sadness.*
>
> —Antoine de Saint-Exupéry

When I experience sadness, envy, anger, or any other painful emotion, I remind myself that these emotions are natural, part of being a healthy human being. When I reject painful emotions, when I don't allow myself to experience them naturally, they expand and intensify. Moreover, when I do not allow myself to experience emotions like sorrow, fear, or hatred, I limit my capacity for joy, happiness, and love. All feelings flow along the same emotional pipeline, and when I block one set of emotions (the painful ones), I am also indirectly blocking others (the pleasurable ones).

Painful emotions are an inevitable part of the experience of being human, and therefore when I reject them I am, in fact, rejecting part of my humanity. To lead a full and fulfilling life—a happy life—I need to allow myself to experience the full range of human emotions. I need to give myself permission to be human.[97]

THE BEST ADVICE THAT my wife, Tami, and I received when David, our first child, was born came from our pediatrician. "Over the next few months," he said, "you're going to experience a whole range of emotions, often to the extreme. You're going to experience joy and awe, frustration and anger, happiness and irritation. This is normal. We all go through it." Was he right! While there certainly were moments of joy, there were difficult moments, too.

When David was a month old, I started to feel some envy toward him. Why? Because for the first time since Tami and I started dating, she was focusing most of her attention on someone else rather than on me. But then five minutes after feeling envy, I would experience the most intense love toward David. My initial reaction was to view myself as a hypocrite, to question the authenticity of my love: How could my feelings of love for him be real if at the same time I also envied him? And then our pediatrician's words came to mind, reminding me that it was natural to feel what I was feeling. He had given me permission to be human.

The doctor's advice helped me in two related ways. First, because I recognized and accepted—rather than rejected and suppressed—my feeling of envy, it gradually subsided and lost its hold. Second, I was able to experience and enjoy the feeling of love much more intensely—without its being spoiled by feelings of guilt or disingenuousness.

Allow all emotions, the painful and the pleasurable, to flow through you. Celebrate your humanity.

98.

BE UNGENEROUS

—or—

Act generously

> *Thousands of candles can be lighted from a single candle, and the life of the candle will not be shortened. Happiness never decreases by being shared.*
>
> —SIDDHARTHA GAUTAMA BUDDHA

SO MANY PEOPLE OPERATE under the assumption—whether consciously or not—that when they give something away without getting immediate and tangible rewards in return, they lose out. Their worldview revolves around the notion that the size of the pie is fixed, and therefore, another's gain is necessarily their loss. What they fail to recognize is that there's so much benefit to the person who gives, that I often think there is no more selfish act than a generous act.

There are four ways in which being generous contributes to my welfare. First, each act of generosity is a small contribution toward making the world a better and more pleasant place to live in. Second, through empathy, seeing the recipients of my generosity happy increases my own happiness, too. Third, good deeds tend to be rewarded, not just in terms of the way I feel, but also in terms of tangible success. Fourth, recognizing that my action contributes to the world makes life worth living: All of us need to feel that we are creating value, that we are, in some way, making the world a better place.[98]

THOSE WHO GIVE GENEROUSLY are, ultimately, more successful. For example, the most successful managers are the ones who are generous with their knowledge. In contrast, managers who do not share their experience and expertise with their employees because they are afraid of competition are less successful. Generous managers do not feel threatened by their employees; they recruit the best people they can find to work under them, and then help their employees to develop even further. Consequently, these managers are able to deliver better results, succeed more, and take on more responsibility.

In my work as an organizational behaviorist, I have often seen how the success of managers is directly correlated to their generosity—how talented managers undermine their own progress by keeping their knowledge to themselves, and how other managers rise to greater prominence through giving. Acting generously as a way of life is, in the long run, beneficial to everyone.

While the rewards of generosity do often come in the form of material success, they always pay dividends in the currency of happiness. Happiness is an unlimited resource—there is no fixed pie, and one person's gain is not another person's loss. Through our generosity we can tap the infinite reserve of spiritual and emotional wealth.

Give yourself the gift of giving.

99.

LOOK FOR THE QUICK FIX

—*or*—

Have patience

> *Progress is relatively fast in fields that apply knowledge to the material world, such as physics or genetics. But it is painfully slow when knowledge is to be applied to modify our own habits and desires.*
>
> —Mihaly Csikszentmihalyi

In Hebrew, the words *sevel* (suffering), *sibolet* (endurance), and *savlanut* (patience) stem from the same root. To develop and grow we must learn to be patient, to endure, and that sometimes entails suffering. The expectation that personal change is effortless and fast is a sure way to disappointment and frustration.

In his work on intimacy, David Schnarch points to the importance of "meaningful endurance" as a way to frame the difficulties that are part and parcel of every thriving long-term relationship. The couple has to endure hardship, and that often entails suffering; however, the process is meaningful in that it potentially leads to a deeper and better connection. The same patience, the same meaningful endurance, is necessary for any change process—to enjoy positive change individually, interpersonally, and organizationally.[99]

I HEARD THE FOLLOWING story in a parenting workshop run by the Adler Institute in Israel. A woman was shopping in a supermarket when her young child started to cry. The woman, in a calm voice, said, "We just need to get a few more things, Sharon, and then we're done." The tantrum continued, the child screaming even louder. The mother said calmly, "We've finished shopping, Sharon; all we need to do is to pay."

At the cashier, the screaming and crying intensified. The mother, still quiet and collected, continued, "We are almost done, Sharon, and then we can go to the car." The child continued screaming until finally they got to the car and she calmed down.

A young man came over to the mother and said to her, "I watched you in there, and I just wanted to tell you how impressed I am with your ability to keep your calm while Sharon was throwing her tantrum. I learned an important lesson from you."

The mother thanked the man, and then added: "But her name is not Sharon. I am Sharon."

100.

SUCCUMB TO THE TEDIUM

—or—

Find the extraordinary in the ordinary

The invariable mark of wisdom is to see the miraculous in the common.

—Ralph Waldo Emerson

Wherever I look, I can find the miraculous—even in the very act of looking! While science can describe vision—how light rays form images in my visual cortex or how each neuron has a specialized function—it does not explain how or why it is that I see, or what is the *I* that sees. The seemingly ordinary fact that I am conscious and aware right now is in fact extraordinary, a miracle that science cannot explain. At every moment in my life I can choose to be conscious of the fact that there is nothing ordinary about being alive. If I take the time to look—to really look—at a person, or a tree, or a car, then I can see that nothing is or can be dull. How interesting, how fascinating, this world is![100]

I WAS TWENTY-SEVEN YEARS old, living in Singapore, working at a shipping company as an organizational behaviorist. It was the end of another long day at work and, as I had done so many times before, I crossed a bridge on my way home. Until that day, the bridge was just another obstacle to cross on the way to my destination. But that day, things changed. Or rather, I changed.

I climbed the bridge and reached the top, slightly out of breath, when suddenly, I was struck. I looked around me and saw stones, trees, and birds. I saw billboards, lights, skyscrapers, and cars. I saw people, and I saw myself: standing there in the midst of it all, consciously observing, thinking, reflecting, and, for the first time, recognizing.

Until that day I never took special notice of the wonder that was unfolding around me and within me. Every day I encountered the same bridge, the same landscape, and the numbing force of repetition blinded me to what I was actually seeing. "If the stars should appear one night in a thousand years," says Emerson, "how would men believe and adore; and preserve for many generations the remembrance of the city of God." But because the stars appear every night, because trees grow all around us, we take the "city of God" for granted. But on that day I grasped that I was part of a miracle. Familiarity may have desensitized me to the miracle, but it could not make it go away.

As you cross bridges, watch the stars, look into the eyes of a stranger, or close your eyes and meditate, remember that at every moment in your life, you can choose to see.

101.

DISMISS DREAMS

—or—

Take dreams seriously

Shoot for the moon.
Even if you miss you'll land among the stars.
—Les Brown

Voices around us abound, urging us to drop our dreams and become realistic. Some of these voices are friendly ones, belonging to people who truly care about us—and who do not want us to get hurt, to be disappointed. And indeed, low expectations may reduce the likelihood of discontent in the shorter term. However, low expectations also prevent us from getting to places that are within our reach, and ultimately lead to more unhappiness because we know that we have not stretched ourselves and realized our potential. Even if we fail to fulfill the particular dream we had, we're likely to expand our horizon, reach new territories, and turn other dreams into reality.

Pursuing our dreams is what life is really all about.[101]

MY PARENTS ALWAYS TOOK my dreams seriously. When, as a child, I told my dad of my interest in a topic—be it engineering, geography, embroidery, psychology, music, or aeronautics—he immediately exposed me to the latest thinking in that field. Even if these interests changed faster than the clothes on a runway model, he would spend as much time as I desired indulging my passion du jour.

My mom is no different. When my brother and I declared that we wanted to be squash champions, she joined us on the journey—never pushing, and never withdrawing her support. We did not reach our dream—we wanted to be world champions, the "Williams brothers" of the squash world—and yet between us, we won a fair number of national championships. More important, we learned about the value of hard work and dedication to a goal, about dealing with challenges and failures and triumphs; and most of all, we learned that our dreams matter.

This morning I told my mom about my latest dream—to create an online master's degree in positive psychology that will attract students who want to make the world a better place. Whether I'll pursue this path, time will tell, but a few hours later, my mom called and told me that she's been thinking about my idea, and offered a number of suggestions for what the program can include. She's taking my dream seriously, as she always does.

I am dedicating this book to my parents, because without them I doubt that I would have realized my dream of becoming a writer.

I have a choice

—and—

I choose to choose

Choice unleashes the potential within each moment.

❋ ❋ ❋

As you become mindful of the potential within this moment,
your life gains momentum,
becomes momentous.

❋ ❋ ❋

When a moment matters, life matters.

Acknowledgments

WRITING IS MY PASSION, and I am grateful for having chosen to become a writer. I am even more grateful for the people who have become part of my life as a result of my chosen profession. Kim Cooper and Adam Vital have worked with me on this book from its idea phase to its final version. They are, in Ralph Waldo Emerson's definition of the ideal friend, my beautiful enemies—challenging me, pushing me, making me a better writer and thinker.

Whenever I have an idea for a book, the first person I turn to is Rafe Sagalyn of The Sagalyn Agency. His advice throughout the long process of writing is always wise and enlightening. Particularly, his advice to publish this book with The Experiment has been among the best he has given me. Working with Matthew Lore, Cara Bedick, and their team has been professionally and personally rewarding.

C.J. Lonoff of Speaking Matters has for the past decade paved the way for many of the things that I do, and it excites me to think of the roads we'll continue to travel together.

I am deeply indebted to Ellen Langer, whose seminal research on the topic of choice influenced my thinking in significant ways. Her work on this topic was—and continues to be—revolutionary. I am indebted, too, to the work of the many psychologists I cite in this book, especially to Edward Deci, Sheena Iyengar, Sonja Lyubomirsky, Karen Reivich, Richard Ryan, Barry Schwartz, Martin Seligman, and Kennon Sheldon.

Numerous conversations with Rami Ziv have given birth to many of the choices I present in this book—as well as to the choice I made to become a psychologist and philosopher.

Pninit Russo-Netzer and Jorge Perelman read through the manuscript and provided valuable feedback.

Zevik and Aterett, beyond being the best brother and sister one could ask for, are exceptionally insightful and constantly contribute to my writing and thinking. I am also grateful for my sister's choice to bring Udi Mozes into our family—his professionalism in our work together is surpassed only by his kindness and generosity.

To have met Tami at the age of fourteen is, to my mind, the luckiest break I've ever had. To decide to spend my life with her—and to raise three wonderful children together—is the best choice I've ever made.

This book is dedicated to my amazing parents. It is only now, as a parent myself, that I fully grasp the sometimes overwhelming number of choices that have to be made when raising children. I will be forever grateful for the paths they chose to take.

I am writing these lines on a transatlantic flight from Tel Aviv to New York. Before I began, I felt drained—exhausted after a particularly long and demanding day of work which was followed by an equally difficult night of tending to one of my children who was unwell. But as soon as I started to reflect on all the people to whom I am grateful—those who are acknowledged here by name and the many more to whom I owe thanks—I felt reinvigorated and my energies were renewed. This reminded me, yet again, of how the simple choices we make every moment can have a far-reaching effect on the way we experience our life, and how one of the best choices we can make is to express gratitude for all we have to be grateful for.

Notes

1. R. M. LeGault. *Think! Why Crucial Decisions Can't Be Made in the Blink of an Eye* (New York: Threshold Editions, 2006).

2. J. Kabat-Zinn. *Full Catastrophe Living: Using the Wisdom of Your Body and Mind to Face Stress, Pain, and Illness* (New York: Delta, 1990).

3. D. Goleman. *Emotional Intelligence: Why It Can Matter More Than IQ* (New York: Bantam, 2006).

4. J. M. G. Williams. *The Mindful Way Through Depression: Freeing Yourself from Chronic Unhappiness* (New York: The Guilford Press, 2007).

5. N. Branden. *The Six Pillars of Self-Esteem: The Definitive Work on Self-Esteem by the Leading Pioneer in the Field* (New York: Bantam, 1994).

6. R. E. Quinn. *Change the World: How Ordinary People Can Achieve Extraordinary Results* (San Francisco: Jossey-Bass, 2000).

7. A. Ellis and W. J. Knaus. *Overcoming Procrastination: Or How to Think and Act Rationally in Spite of Life's Inevitable Hassles* (New York: Signet, 1979).

8. R. D. Enright. *Forgiveness Is a Choice: A Step-by-Step Process for Resolving Anger and Restoring Hope,* APA Lifetools (Washington, DC: American Psychological Association, 2001).

9. D. William. *The Path to Purpose: How Young People Find Their Calling in Life* (New York: Free Press, 2009).

10. L. G. Calhoun and R. G. Tedeschi. *The Handbook of Posttraumatic Growth: Research and Practice* (Mahwah, NJ: Lawrence Erlbaum Associates, 2006).

11. Dalai Lama. *An Open Heart: Practicing Compassion in Everyday Life* (New York: Back Bay Books, 2002).

12. P. J. Palmer. *The Courage to Teach: Exploring the Inner Landscape of a Teacher's Life,* 10th Anniversary Edition (San Francisco: Jossey-Bass, 2007).

13. S. R. Covey. *The 7 Habits of Highly Effective People* (New York: Free Press, 2004).

14. C. Honoré. *In Praise of Slowness: Challenging the Cult of Speed* (San Francisco: HarperOne, 2005).

15. D. Buettner. *The Blue Zones: Lessons for Living Longer from the People Who've Lived the Longest* (Washington, DC: National Geographic, 2010).

16. R. Wiseman. *The Luck Factor: The Four Essential Principles* (New York: Miramax, 2004).

17. J. M. Schwartz and R. Gladding. *You Are Not Your Brain: The 4-Step Solution for Changing Bad Habits, Ending Unhealthy Thinking, and Taking Control of Your Life* (New York: Avery, 2011).

18. T. Roth. *How Full Is Your Bucket? Positive Strategies for Work and Life* (New York: Gallup Press, 2004).

19. T. Ben-Shahar. *Being Happy: You Don't Have to Be Perfect to Lead a Richer, Happier Life* (New York: McGraw-Hill, 2010).

20. C. R. Rogers. *On Becoming a Person: A Therapist's View of Psychotherapy* (Boston: Mariner Books, 1995).

21. T. Kasser. *The High Price of Materialism* (Cambridge, MA: Bradford Books, MIT Press, 2003).

22. A. C. L. Huang. *Mentoring: The Tao of Giving and Receiving Wisdom* (San Francisco: HarperOne, 1995).

23. W. Ury. *Getting Past No* (New York: Bantam, 1993).

24. AA World Services. *Alcoholics Anonymous Comes of Age: A Brief History of AA* (New York: Alcoholics Anonymous World Services, 1970).

25. K. R. Jamison. *Exuberance: The Passion for Life* (New York: Vintage, 2005).

26. D. Kahneman. *Thinking, Fast and Slow* (New York: Farrar, Straus and Giroux, 2011).

27. L. Piekoff and A. Rand. *Introduction to Objectivist Epistemology* (New York: Plume, 1990).

28. I. D. Yalom. *Existential Psychotherapy* (New York: Basic Books, 1980).

29. C. R. Snyder. *The Psychology of Hope: You Can Get Here from There* (New York: Free Press, 1994).

30. A. Kohn. *Punished by Rewards: The Trouble with Gold Stars, Incentive Plans, A's, Praise, and Other Bribes* (Boston: Mariner Books, 1999).

31. D. O. Clifton and M. Buckingham. *Now, Discover Your Strengths* (New York: Free Press, 2001).

32. H. Benson and E. M. Stuart. *Wellness Book: The Comprehensive Guide to Maintaining Health and Treating Stress-Related Illness* (New York: Scribner, 1993).

33. C. S. Dweck. *Mindset: The New Psychology of Success* (New York: Ballantine Books, 2007).

34. M. Müller. *Wisdom of the Buddha: The Unabridged Dhammapada* (New York: Cosimo Classics, 2007).

35. J. J. Ratey. *Spark: The Revolutionary New Science of Exercise and the Brain* (New York: Little, Brown and Company, 2008).

36. E. J. Langer. *The Power of Mindful Learning* (Cambridge, MA: Da Capo Press, 1998).

37. P. Schmuck and M. S. Kennon. *Life Goals and Well-Being: Towards a Positive Psychology of Human Striving* (Kirkland, WA: Hogrefe & Huber Publishing, 2001).

38. D. D. Burns. *The Feeling Good Handbook* (New York: Plume, 1999).

39. R. B. Zajonc. *The Selected Works of R. B. Zajonc* (Hoboken, NJ: Wiley, 2003).

40. D. L. Cooperrider and D. Whitney. *Appreciative Inquiry: A Positive Revolution in Change* (San Francisco: Berrett-Koehler Publishers, 2005).

41. J. Kabat-Zinn. *Wherever You Go, There You Are* (New York: Hyperion, 2005).

42. P. Bloom. *How Pleasure Works: The New Science of Why We Like What We Like* (New York: W. W. Norton & Company, 2011).

43. T. Ben-Shahar. *Happier: Learn the Secrets to Daily Joy and Lasting Fulfillment* (New York: McGraw-Hill, 2007).

44. T. Ben-Shahar. *Being Happy: You Don't Have to Be Perfect to Lead a Richer, Happier Life* (New York: McGraw-Hill, 2010).

45. S. Lyubomirsky. *The How of Happiness: A New Approach to Getting the Life You Want* (New York: Penguin, 2008).

46. T. Crum. *Three Deep Breaths: Finding Power and Purpose in a Stressed-Out World* (San Francisco: Berrett-Koehler Publishers, 2009).

47. J. M. Gottman. J. S. Gottman, and J. DeClaire, *Ten Lessons to Transform Your Marriage: America's Love Lab Experts Share Their Strategies for Strengthening Your Relationship* (New York: Three Rivers Press, 2007).

48. R. W. Emerson. *Essays: First Series* (Seattle, WA: CreateSpace, 2011).

49. C. Peterson and M. Seligman. *Character Strengths and Virtues: A Handbook and Classification* (New York: Oxford University Press, 2004).

50. R. Emmons. *Thanks! How Practicing Gratitude Can Make You Happier* (New York: Mariner Books, 2008).

51. G. Prochnik. *In Pursuit of Silence: Listening for Meaning in a World of Noise* (New York: Anchor, 2011).

52. W. Bennis. *On Becoming a Leader* (New York: Basic Books, 2009).

53. G. H. Mead. *Selected Writings* (Chicago: University of Chicago Press, 1981).

54. B. Schwartz. *The Paradox of Choice: Why More Is Less* (New York: Harper Perennial, 2005).

55. T. Brach. *Radical Acceptance: Embracing Your Life with the Heart of a Buddha* (New York: Bantam, 2004).

56. Heraclitus and G. S. Kirk. *Heraclitus: The Cosmic Fragments* (New York: Cambridge University Press, 2010).

57. M. Ricard. *Art of Meditation* (London: Atlantic Books, 2010).

58. D. Goleman. *Destructive Emotions: A Scientific Dialogue with the Dalai Lama* (New York: Bantam, 2004).

59. J. E. Loehr and T. Schwartz. *The Power of Full Engagement: Managing Energy, Not Time, Is the Key to High Performance and Personal Renewal* (New York: Free Press, 2004).

60. V. E. Frankl. *Man's Search for Meaning* (Boston: Beacon Press, 2006).

61. J. T. Cacioppo, E. Hatfield, and R. L. Rapson. *Emotional Contagion, Studies in Emotion and Social Interaction* (New York: Cambridge University Press, 1993).

62. J. W. Pennebaker. *Opening Up: The Healing Power of Expressing Emotions* (New York: Guilford Press, 1997).

63. S. Pinker. *The Blank Slate: The Modern Denial of Human Nature* (New York: Penguin, 2003).

64. M. Collins. *Ordinary Children, Extraordinary Teachers* (San Francisco: Hampton Roads Publishing, 1992).

65. P. G. Zimbardo and J. Boyd. *The Time Paradox: The New Psychology of Time That Will Change Your Life* (New York: Free Press, 2009).

66. S. R. Peterson and R. L. Bednar. *Self-Esteem: Paradoxes and Innovations in Clinical Theory and Practice* (Washington, DC: American Psychological Association, 1995).

67. M. H. Kernis. *Self-Esteem Issues and Answers: A Sourcebook of Current Perspectives* (New York: Psychology Press, 2006).

68. T. Ben-Shahar. *Happier: Learn the Secrets to Daily Joy and Lasting Fulfillment* (New York: McGraw-Hill, 2007).

69. O. Sachs. *Musicophilia: Tales of Music and the Brain* (New York: Vintage, 2008).

70. K. Reivich and A. Shatte. *The Resilience Factor: 7 Keys to Finding Your Inner Strength and Overcoming Life's Hurdles* (New York: Three Rivers Press, 2003).

71. J. S. Mill. *The Subjection of Women* (Seattle, WA: CreateSpace, 2011).

72. A. H. Maslow. *The Farther Reaches of Human Nature* (New York: Penguin/Arkana, 1993).

73. L. Kaplan Thaler and R. Koval. *The Power of Nice: How to Conquer the Business World with Kindness* (New York: Crown Business, 2006).

74. S. Brown and C. Vaughan. *Play: How It Shapes the Brain, Opens the Imagination, and Invigorates the Soul* (New York: Avery Trade, 2010).

75. P. M. Senge. *The Fifth Discipline: The Art and Practice of the Learning Organization* (New York: Crown Business, 2006).

76. P. J. Palmer. *Let Your Life Speak: Listening for the Voice of Vocation* (San Francisco: Jossey-Bass, 1999).

77. M. E. P. Seligman. *Learned Optimism: How to Change Your Mind and Your Life* (New York: Vintage, 2006).

78. B. George. *Authentic Leadership: Rediscovering the Secrets to Creating Lasting Value,* Jossey-Bass Warren Bennis Series (San Francisco: Jossey-Bass, 2004).

79. D. Schnarch. *Passionate Marriage: Keeping Love and Intimacy Alive in Committed Relationships* (New York: W. W. Norton & Company, 2009).

80. E. J. Langer. *Mindfulness* (Cambridge, MA: Da Capo Press, A Merloyd Lawrence Book, 1990).

81. B. Fredrickson. *Positivity: Groundbreaking Research Reveals How to Embrace the Hidden Strength of Positive Emotions, Overcome Negativity, and Thrive* (New York: Crown Archetype, 2009).

82. A. Bandura. *Self-Efficacy: The Exercise of Control* (New York: Worth Publishers, 1997).

83. Aristotle, R. C. Bartlett, and S. D. Collins. *Aristotle's Nicomachean Ethics* (Chicago: University of Chicago Press, 2011).

84. T. J. Thatchenkery and C. Metzker. *Appreciative Intelligence: Seeing the Mighty Oak in the Acorn* (San Francisco: Berrett-Koehler Publishers, 2006).

85. N. Branden. *Honoring the Self: Self-Esteem and Personal Transformation* (New York: Bantam, 1985).

86. N. Branden. *The Six Pillars of Self-Esteem: The Definitive Work on Self-Esteem by the Leading Pioneer in the Field* (New York: Bantam, 1995).

87. H. D. Thoreau. *Walden* (Seattle, WA: CreateSpace, 2012).

88. D. K. Simonton. *Origins of Genius: Darwinian Perspectives on Creativity* (New York: Oxford University Press, 1999).

89. D. Shapiro. *Autonomy and Rigid Character* (New York: Basic Books, 1984).

90. D. Steindl-Rast. *Gratefulness, the Heart of Prayer: An Approach to Life in Fullness* (Ramsey, NJ: Paulist Press, 1990).

91. D. Zohar and I. N. Marshall. *SQ: Connecting with Our Spiritual Intelligence* (New York: Bloomsbury USA, 2001).

92. J. Badaracco. *Leading Quietly* (Boston: Harvard Business Review Press, 2002).

93. A. Faber and E. Mazlish. *How to Talk So Kids Will Listen and Listen So Kids Will Talk* (New York: Scribner, 2012).

94. E. L. Deci and R. M. Ryan. *The Handbook of Self-Determination Research* (Rochester: University of Rochester Press, 2002).

95. E. J. Langer. *On Becoming an Artist: Reinventing Yourself Through Mindful Creativity* (New York: Ballantine Books, 2006).

96. S. L. Orem, J. Binkert, and A. L. Clancy. *Appreciative Coaching: A Positive Process for Change,* Jossey-Bass Business & Management (San Francisco: Jossey-Bass, 2007).

97. T. Ben-Shahar. *Being Happy: You Don't Have to Be Perfect to Lead a Richer, Happier Life* (New York: McGraw-Hill, 2010).

98. Z. Magen. *Exploring Adolescent Happiness: Commitment, Purpose, and Fulfillment* (Thousand Oaks, CA: Sage Publications, 1998).

99. M. E. P. Seligman. *What You Can Change and What You Can't: The Complete Guide to Successful Self-Improvement* (New York: Vintage, 2007).

100. R. W. Emerson. *Nature and Other Writings* (Seattle, WA: CreateSpace, 2010).

101. K. Robinson and L. Aronica. *The Element: How Finding Your Passion Changes Everything* (New York: Penguin, 2009).

About the Author

TAL BEN-SHAHAR, PHD, is an author and lecturer. His classes on "Positive Psychology" and "The Psychology of Leadership" were among the largest courses in Harvard's history, attracting a total of 1,400 students per semester—approximately 20 percent of all Harvard undergraduates. Author of *Happier: Learn the Secrets to Daily Joy and Lasting Fulfillment*, Ben-Shahar consults and lectures around the world on happiness, self-esteem, resilience, goal setting, mindfulness, and leadership. He holds a PhD in organizational behavior and a BA in philosophy and psychology from Harvard.